Paul Bowles by His Friends

Books by Paul Bowles

Fiction

Call at Corazon
Let It Come Down
Midnight Mass
Pages from Cold Point
The Sheltering Sky
The Spider's House
A Thousand Days for Mokhtar
Up Above the World

Non-Fiction

Points in Time
Their Heads Are Green
Two Years Beside the Strait: Tangier Journal 1987–9
Without Stopping

By Jane Bowles

The Collected Works of Jane Bowles
Plain Pleasures

Paul Bowles
by His Friends

Edited & with an Introduction by
Gary Pulsifer

Peter Owen · *London*

PETER OWEN PUBLISHERS
73 Kenway Road London SW5 0RE

First published in Great Britain 1992
© the contributors and Peter Owen Limited 1992

A catalogue record for this book is available from
the British Library

ISBN 0–7206–0866–X

Printed and bound in Great Britain

Contents

Illustrations

(on pages 20 to 25)

Acknowledgements

We are indebted to the publishers, editors, broadcasters and authors concerned for permission to adapt and reprint the following:

William S. Burroughs and Francis Bacon: 'Art, Death and Immortality over a Naked Lunch' (BBC TV's *Arena* programme, unused footage, 1986)

Melvyn Bragg: 'Listing to Port' (*Punch*, 12 August 1981)

Patricia Highsmith: 'Patricia Highsmith Recalls a North African Encounter' (*Vogue*, August 1989)

Nicholas Lezard: 'Living Alone on the Fringes of Literature' (*The Sunday Correspondent*, 8 July 1990)

Richard Rayner: 'Relishing the Abyss and the Furies' (*Sunday Telegraph*, 6 August 1989)

John Ryle: 'A Refuge in the Shadows of the Tangier Casbah' (*The Independent on Sunday*, 24 June 1990)

Gore Vidal: Introduction to *Collected Stories of Paul Bowles* (Santa Rosa, Calif.: Black Sparrow Press, 1983)

I should like to express my gratitude to my parents, Donald and Carol Pulsifer, and to Lorna Starbird for their support over the years. Thanks are also due to Peter Owen, who welcomed my initial idea for this book; Michael Levien, for his superb in-house editing; James Grauerholtz of William S. Burroughs Communications; and Rupert Haselden and Nigel Finch, producer of *Arena*. A special thank you to Richard Bates of Discript Ltd, with whom I first met Paul Bowles, and to all those others who so generously contributed to this book.

Gary Pulsifer

Introduction

This tribute to Paul Bowles has been written by Paul Bowles's *friends*, in the widest sense of the word. Some of the contributors – writers, painters, composers, journalists and publishers – have known Mr Bowles for a good many years, while for others the acquaintance has been more cursory. Some, like Edouard Roditi and Stephen Spender, knew Paul Bowles in thirties' Berlin, while Beats such as William Burroughs, Allen Ginsberg and Gregory Corso came across him in Tangier during the fifties.

Patricia Highsmith knew Paul and Jane Bowles in New York, and became reacquainted with Paul a few years ago in Tangier, staying in Jane Bowles's old apartment below Paul's. This apartment until recently belonged to Buffie Johnson, who writes about Paul and the literary avant garde in New York City. James Purdy also met Paul Bowles in New York, in the company of Carl Van Vechten. Another old friend is Gore Vidal, as is David Herbert , social arbiter of Tangier's expatriate community. David Herbert once had a pact with Jane Bowles that if anything happened to Paul, they would marry.

Lady St Just, together with her great friend Tennessee Williams, saw Paul in Rome and she talks about Tennessee Williams's influence on Paul Bowles the man and the writer. Two of Paul Bowles's publishers, Peter Owen and Lawrence Ferlinghetti, pay tribute, while the novelist and broadcaster Melvyn Bragg, who went to Tangier to film a *South Bank Show* programme on Paul, writes about *The Sheltering Sky*.

The composers Ned Rorem and Phillip Ramey discuss Paul's musical compositions. Mr Ramey also provides an original composition for piano, 'Portrait: Paul Bowles at Eighty', while John Cage contributes something of a musical tribute. Charles Henri Ford has written a haiku for 'Paul Frederic Bowles'.

9

Marguerite McBey, a long-time resident of Tangier, painted both Paul and Jane, and here she looks back at several encounters with the Bowleses. Joseph McPhillips, of the American School in Tangier, records his theatrical collaborations with Paul. Gavin Young, a comparatively recent habitué of Tangier, reveals a playful side to Paul Bowles's character.

Millicent Dillon interviewed Paul while researching her biography of Jane Bowles: she is now at work on a biography of Paul. Ira Cohen and John Hopkins, in journal extracts, record their friendship with Paul, while Terry Wilson spotlights the legendary Mr Bowles during a crowded visit to his apartment. Both John Ryle and Nicholas Lezard journeyed to Tangier to interview Mr Bowles, respectively for *The Independent on Sunday* and *The Sunday Correspondent*.

Gavin Lambert met Paul Bowles in California, at the home of Christopher Isherwood and Don Bachardy. The poet Ruth Fainlight went to Tangier with her husband Alan Sillitoe, became friendly with the Bowleses and then returned with her young family. Richard Rayner provides a biographical and critical appraisal of the Bowleses. Anne Cumming returned to Tangier bearing a jar containing the ashes of Brion Gysin, her adopted brother. She writes movingly about scattering Brion's ashes with Paul and several others on the cliffs overlooking Cap Spartel. The Spanish writer Emilio Sanz de Soto ruminates on a friendship going back many years and recalls some of their creative friends.

What emerges is a composite picture of the sometimes elusive Paul Bowles the man, the writer and the composer. We hope it will please Mr Bowles, the friend.

Gary Pulsifer

10

Melvyn Bragg

Listing to Port

Paul Bowles is one of those legendary figures very few people know about. Oh yes – American, exile, friend of all that mighty, post-Second World War flood of international American writers, the author in the North African gardens of strangeness and sensuality, the desert guide, elegant, aloof, a 'writer's writer'. Rather like Henry Green in England, he carries that dubious compliment, 'the writer's writer' – dubious because I have always felt that it was ultimately patronizing and ambiguous, generally meaning that you liked the guy very much and were almost embarrassed that so few others liked the writing.

This is, strictly speaking, unfair to Bowles, whose travel books, stories, autobiography and translations from Arabic have made him not only a name but a living, and what more could a writer desire? The name indeed crops up all over the shop. Few English-speaking writers have been to North Africa without seeking out Bowles or being brought to him. The reputation is here on the dust-jacket of his first novel, now republished. He is almost outrageously hung about with medals, like some Audie Murphy of the book-war: 'A novel touched with genius . . .', 'Now and then, perhaps once in five years a novel appears . . .', 'Like Virgil and Dante before him he has the common compassion to go to hell with the children of his imagination', 'At his best, Bowles has no peer. . . .'

The Sheltering Sky was first published in 1949. It tells the story of an American couple, Port and his wife Kit, who are travellers. The distinction is early made between travellers and tourists. Tourists come and go: travellers stay and go on. Port has inherited some money and with it a disdain for the world as represented by the second war; he is the archetypal seeker for the innocent state, the stainless past, the Eden, as he imagines it, of pre-mechanized man. Kit goes along with him. In her life what matters is the power of luck, the sense of magical forces which deliver omens in commonplace encounters; this beguiling idea is, alas, undernourished and soon Kit becomes not much more than a drifter.

Joining them – for no strong reason – on their travels is a younger American, Tunner, whose chief preoccupation (though that is not too pressing) is to get into bed with Kit. And near the beginning of their journey they encounter an English couple, mother and snobbish son, who seem to zigzag around Africa looking for material for her books.

The book is compulsively readable, as they say, and yet, despite some melodramatic events, the characters are acted upon rather than acting for themselves. Port, for example, in his determination to put himself at the mercy of his most obscure whim and instinct, will drift dangerously into an encounter with a desert tribe and decide, despite the obvious risk, to take the proffered girl – with the inevitable consequences of attempted theft, alarums, hullabaloo, a chase, escape – and yet we do not *feel* for him or *with* him. Perhaps that is Mr Bowles's point. Kit drunkenly accedes to Tunner's clumsy overtures and yet in her 'betrayal' we feel no loss; nor do we feel that Tunner has gained anything. Which is not to say the characters are lifeless; not at all. They are just somehow surface painted; the deeper motivations which would have preoccupied D.H. Lawrence are unspoken.

The Lawrentian analogy is useful, for the book develops into the classic confrontation between Western and deceptively primitive customs. Port, who eschews medicines, contracts typhoid and dies. Kit, alarmed, though apparently not deeply upset by this, runs even further south, even deeper into the desert, and is picked up by an Arab caravan whose black-bearded leader ravishes her, maltreats her and imprisons her. When she does finally escape, she has gone mad.

It is difficult to know what to make of it. Certainly the descriptions of the places themselves are marvellous and meticulous. Whether Bowles is writing about garbage, flies, the desert, the Casbah, Arab traders, markets, hotels, bedrooms, trains, canals, smells – he employs a concentrated certainty of prose which is most impressive. You feel he could reach out and tell you anything about that place, its look, its feel, its ways – and yet the net effect is of an intensely meshed, impenetrable surface. Not that he is superficial, not for a moment. But the way of seeking is as much that of a photographer as a novelist. So detailed and finely written, though, that for the descriptions alone the book is worth reading.

Mailer said that Bowles 'opened the world of Hip'. That dates us all. But if it is to be traced in *The Sheltering Sky* then we see its first fingers pointing to a world of arbitrary action, wilful risk-taking – more than that, a willingness freely to enter into an action whose consequences can in no way be calculated. The ideas of magic and chance became the ruling deities. The wilfulness of Lawrence, the determination to explore, to change, to discover, is diminished: the game is to be like chaff, blown in the wind, attentive to the impulse which will very often be destructive as it is here.

In *The Sheltering Sky* Bowles's characters put themselves outside accepted moralities, their own and those of others, and stand prepared to be discounted. It is an experiment in living which could be called utterly effete, self-centred and pointless. It does not move us because it seems so little to move them. Yet we feel that the author is showing us a world whose meaninglessness has been somehow penetrated. In that sense, it is so cool it freezes the blood.

William S. Burroughs

Paul Bowles is one of the most impeccably, almost inhumanly reserved men I have ever known, reminiscent of the subject of Edwin Arlington Robinson's poem, 'The Man Flamonde' – 'How was it that his charm revealed/Somehow the surface of a shield?'

His writing is equally distinguished and special – the typhoid dream from *The Sheltering Sky* and the hashish delirium at the dead-end of *Let It Come Down* – these are among my favourite passages in contemporary writing.

The end of *The Sheltering Sky* is a classic that can take its rightful place alongside the end of Fitzgerald's *The Great Gatsby* or the end of Joyce's story, 'The Dead'. As the crazed nymphomaniac Kit wanders away into the Native Quarter, the streetcar 'made a wide U-turn and stopped; it was the end of the line'. According to Bernardo Bertolucci, whose film version of *The Sheltering Sky* was released in late 1990, this ending is too heavy a note of despair for the visual end of a film; but for a book, it is masterful.

There is about Paul's writing, at its best, a palpable darkness, like underexposed film, that fills the narrow North African streets, always darker and darkening. . . . I am forever indebted to Paul, for his writing, which drew me to Tangier in 1953; and for his cherished friendship, then and since. I salute him at eighty-two years, as I did at forty-five.

William S. Burroughs and Francis Bacon

Art, Death and Immortality over a Naked Lunch

In 1986, while filming with BBC TV's *Arena*, William Burroughs renewed his old friendship with Francis Bacon at the painter's South Kensington studio. The conversation between these two giants of the art and literary worlds was recorded but never made it to the screen and until now has lain forgotten on a shelf. They had first known each other in Tangier in the 1950s.

W.B.: Have you been back to Tangier?

F.B.: No, never. Did you ever know Peter Lacey?

W.B.: Oh, of course.

F.B.: Well, you know he died there and I went back once afterwards and . . . but I haven't been back for years. And I was in the south of Spain and I just went across, I went across . . . well, I really only just went across for the day. You feel like going back?

W.B.: Oh no, not at all. . . . The last time I was in Tangier must have been in 1973. I was there on an assignment from *Oui* magazine to do something on the Joujouka festival. Did you ever get to Joujouka by the way? Well, that really is fascinating. Worth seeing.

F.B.: Is that the one, that town near Fez . . . that's not the festival they have in a town near Fez, is it?

W.B.: No, this is, let's see, it's about a hundred and fifty miles south of Tangier, you know . . . about fifteen miles, twenty miles inland. That's where they sew the boy into the goat's skin. The rites of Pan . . . that obviously came from Rome. Well, I was there in 1973 and it was quite pleasant, but now it's a million people. That's just happened in the last few years. And this tremendous expansion like they had in Mexico City, you know. It's awful. It's very expensive.

F.B.: But that must be a rite that has moved around the

15

Mediterranean. I mean it must have . . . I don't know where it came from, whether it came from Greece, Turkey . . . but it must have come from the southern or the eastern Mediterranean, I suppose, and it's moved around into Morocco. Probably.

W.B.: No, I really have no desire to go back.

F.B.: No, I don't really.

W.B.: Well, you know, if the place you used to like is changed for the worse it really is sad.

F.B.: Although I like Moroccans.

W.B.: Yes, yes, I like Moroccans.

F.B.: I did like them very much.

W.B.: I don't know why Paul continues to live there.

F.B.: Does Ahmed ever go back? Does Yacoubi ever go back?

W.B.: I don't think so. I saw Yacoubi in New York. He lives right round the corner from where I lived in New York. On Great Johns Street. And I was down on the Bowery . . . just a few blocks, and I ran into him every now and then. He's doing very well, I think. He's a good painter . . . there's no doubt about it.

F.B.: He sent me a book he wrote on cookery, and there's one recipe I should follow up, but I never do. It's when you're sixty-four, how to make yourself younger. But it's so elaborate, it would take such a long time to do it you'd be dead before you got the thing cooked. But he was a good . . . I often used to go to with him to the butcher's. He always knew exactly what to buy and everything. But then that's partly because his father, I think, had been one of those kind of . . . not a doctor, but aren't they called . . . known as religious men. You know, they were bound up with the whole Muslim religion in a sense. Ahmed was brought up in that kind of tradition. He was terribly careful about the type of food and everything he bought.

W.B.: Yes, the Spanish always call them *les hombres que risen*, the men who pray. It's sort of an informal clergy. They don't have any regular priests but they do have these old men who spend most of their time praying. I mean, if you pray six times a day it takes up most of your time. And they are sort of an informal clergy. We met in Tangier, didn't we?

F.B.: I met you but I hardly ever saw you, Bill. Very, very occasionally. I met you either with Janie Bowles or with Paul Bowles, I don't know. I wasn't there very much for one thing, and I was only there really just off and on. I used to see a certain amount of Paul and I saw a certain amount of Ahmed, because . . . we got on very well and he used to come round occasionally.

W.B.: I think that you were one of the influences on Ahmed.

F.B.: Do you think so?

W.B.: Yes, as a painter. Not in any bad sense . . .

F.B.: But everybody's influenced by somebody.

W.B.: Well, of course. Like I'm very much influenced by Denton Welch and Conrad. Have you read Denton Welch? I think he's great.

F.B.: I never knew him. I could have known him but you know he died very, very young.

W.B.: He died at the age of thirty-one as a result of complications from that inexplicable accident. He was bicycling down the road and some lady motorist came and ran into him for no ascertainable reason. That was his last book, *A Voice Through a Cloud*, concerning his accident.

F.B.: I remember reading it at the time . . . or soon after his death, but I never knew him.

W.B.: He reminds me in his writing of Jane Bowles in a way. It was such a distinctive style. Just one sentence and you knew nobody but Janie could have written that. I remember a sentence from *Plain Pleasures*. This old man who had started raising alligators and he said but there was no security in the alligators.

F.B.: Perfect. Marvellous, yes. Well, she certainly pulled out . . . she'd got an alligator round her in Tangier. She'd got a real alligator round her in Tangier . . .

W.B.: A small one? Did it grow to any size? If they reach it, they're delicate things. If they reach a certain size, about that big, then they will live. But usually they die. I had several in my childhood.

F.B.: Because she died here you know, Janie, in a hospital . . . I think it was in Nottingham.

W.B.: Didn't she die in Malaga?

F.B.: You're right, you're absolutely right. She was here though for quite a long time.

W.B.: I think she got shock therapy, which seemed to me a very bad idea but if there's any suggestion of a stroke or any kind of organic brain damage shock therapy is . . .

F.B.: Have you ever known anybody shock therapy did anything for?

W.B.: No.

F.B.: I've known several people and it's never been the slightest bit of good. I mean they've given it up now, more or less.

W.B.: It's used very very seldom. Just when they don't know what else to do in these terrible depressions and things. But no, I've never known anybody . . .

F.B.: Well, of course her problem was that she was really fundamentally obsessed by Paul, and . . . I mean that was in a sense . . . I often think how all her trouble came about, but then it wasn't his fault . . . I mean, if he was more interested in other people or things that's another thing. But I think she was obsessed by Paul.

W.B.: Well, and Sherifa of course.

F.B.: And Sherifa. But then she took on Sherifa because . . . as a sort of . . . something to do with her life.

W.B.: Absolutely.

F.B.: And then Sherifa gave her so much of that . . .

W.B.: *Majoun*? Oh no, she never took *majoun* . . . never . . .

F.B.: No, it wasn't that . . . it wasn't that. It was an old English drug, an old drug that's been going for years . . .

W.B.: Not the stuff that Gandhi . . .

F.B.: It's much used, I believe, in Morocco. It was used by Moroccan women a lot to try and control their husbands . . . with other people. Wish I could think what its name is.

W.B.: It wasn't . . . it was sort of a sedative . . . it wasn't called reserapin? That is supposed to be sort of calming.

F.B.: . . . Well that's one of the things they give for asthma a lot, you see. And . . . it's never done me any good, but that's another story. But no, it was another thing and I cannot think of the name . . . it's stupid, it'll come to me in a moment.

W.B.: She always had a lot of pills around . . . taking pills.

F.B.: Does Paul not like America? Is that the reason he never goes back? Or what is it that keeps him there in Morocco?

W.B.: He doesn't . . . he hates America. Because you know he has this flying thing, he's afraid to fly. Of course you can go by boat, you don't have to fly . . .

F.B.: It's more difficult to go by boat now, isn't it?

W.B.: Well, it can be done. But he is afraid to fly, I don't know why.

F.B.: I used to be for years. I think that's to do with a generation thing. If you're brought up with it you don't think it, but as kids we were brought up in Ireland, you see, and we used to go backwards and forwards between this country and Ireland by boat, so you get used to moving by boat. But I used to hate flying.

W.B.: Well, there's no other way to get around.

F.B.: I believe it's a real game now to get to America by boat.

W.B.: Oh yes, it is. The last time I was on a boat I came back from Tangier in 1964.

Paul Bowles, an early photograph by Allen Ginsberg

One of many watercolour
portraits of Paul Bowles by
Marguerite McBey

Paul Bowles smoking, 1991 (*photograph
Phillip Ramey*)

Gavin Young with Paul Bowles, 1988 (*photograph Phillip Ramey*)

Scattering Brion Gysin's ashes. Paul Bowles and Anne Cumming, January 1986 (*photograph Roberto de Hollanda*)

Paul Bowles with an electronic keyboard at the Grand Hotel Villa de France, Tangier, 1987 (*photograph Phillip Ramey*)

Portrait: Paul Bowles at Eighty
for Piano

Phillip Ramey

June 13, 1991 : Tangier

'Paul Bowles at Eighty', from Phillip Ramey's *Tangier Portraits for Piano*
(1991–2), is freely based on Bowles's Sixth Piano Prelude, strains from
which are transformed harmonically. The piece was given its first
performance by Ramey on 10 July 1991 at the Salle Samuel Beckett, Tangier
(© Phillip Ramey 1991)

Left to right Rodrigo Rey Rosa, Paul Bowles and David Herbert, 1988
(*photograph Phillip Ramey*)

Left to right Krazy Kat, Paul Bowles and Phillip Ramey, 1990
(*photograph Cherie Nutting*)

Paul Bowles with Mohammed Mrabet (*photograph Ira Cohen*)

Left to right Paul Bowles with Raphael Alladin Cohen, Phillip Ramey and Terry Wilson (*photograph Ira Cohen*)

```
          It is  P │ uzzling
             thA │ t
             yoU │ are now
eighty-two years  oL │ d

   all i rememB │ er
    is that yO │ u
            W │ ere
           aL │ ways
  much youngE │ r
your collection of wriS │ t watches
```

Best wishes
John Cage

Ira Cohen

Minbad, Sinbad

'If you are my enemy
I kill you for money
If you are my friend
I kill you for nothing.'

Zocco Chico proverb

Raphael says: 'There are no innocent bystanders.' It's around
3 a.m. at the Grand Hotel Villa de France and we have smoked
almost to the edge of excess. I lie down and close my eyes, listen to
the muezzin. The distant resonances echo in the night of whirling
chakras. The celebratory cries caress the heart of my ear. Remember that my eyes are closed and look into the world of after-image.
Brion Gysin, to the sound of Ben Abou, unrolls the scrolls imprinted on the inner eyelids, there where he proved the theory of
vision. It was then that the Calligraffiti of Fire spoke itself as
Makemono. The patterns on the hotel floor confirm this hypothesis. Brion Gysin proclaimed Master Painter of the after-image
image. His vision was sustained by what he saw. This is his legacy,
the legacy of light. A dog barks as the last muezzin sings.

We go up to see Paul at Immeuble Itesa in Campoamor near the
American Consulate. Up the four flights in the elevator which takes
only three and so Philippe runs up the steps. I ring the bell and
finally the door opens a crack and I see a bent shape in an imaginary
cowl hanging on to the doorknob from below. It is Paul! He is bent
double with sciatica. He smiles in querulous recognition. 'I thought
you were the maid,' he says. 'That's funny,' I reply. 'I thought *you*
were the maid.' We both laugh.

Paul settles on a low couch with difficulty, then repairs to his
bedroom where he props himself up in bed. We talk of Bertolucci

and the filming of *The Sheltering Sky*, and of Debra Winger and John Malkovich. Bertolucci won't let Paul see any rushes. 'Would you let someone look at a half-finished book you are still working on?' Paul sees B's point of view and concurs. B has brought Paul into the film as a 'visible spectator' and has also recorded Paul reading from the book. Paul doesn't know why, says his voice is not interesting. Debra Winger says she will be back to see him in the summer, but Paul dismisses this with a customary fatalism, especially because he clearly looks forward to it. 'Malkovich is very serious, encased within himself,' he says.

I ask Paul how much he's getting paid for the film rights. He shrugs and says 'Nothing'.

Mrabet smokes by himself, hatching black eggs.

The routines are eternal.

The Night Watchmen also watch by day. Time is running in as Raphael writes in his notebook. It is not easy to separate two dogs in the street.

Mrabet tells Paul that the Compania Electrica will come the following morning to change the voltage and Paul speaks of having to put in the plugs. Mrabet says: 'What do you want to plug, el conyo de tu madre?' Paul laughs.

We leave him bibbed and contented with his little table in bed, eating the dinner Mrabet has brought. Everyone is coming to squeeze him dry, but in his own shoulder-shrugging *quien sabe* way he seems to enjoy it.

Philippe reminds me that I should record here that Paul, by his own admission, has never worn earrings. This came up when I gave him a pair of Indonesian Grey parrot earrings which I said perhaps he might like to wear when everyone was gone. When he said 'What?!!' I replied: 'Well, it's never too late. I mean you can always hang them from a lamp or from the moulding.' Once I was bitten by Paul's African grey parrot when I naïvely slipped my finger in through the bars of its cage. That was the parrot rumoured to have died in mysterious circumstances, perhaps even murdered by Sherifa. It often called out 'Allah, Allah'.

Targuisti says Sherifa died more than a year ago. She sold the house Jane bought for her in order to pay the medical bills. He last saw her carrying a basket in the Socco Grande. He mimics Sherifa with crooked face peering up through a squinting eye, telling him: 'I am going to die – I have the cancer. The doctors in Casablanca have all my money and there is nothing to do.'

Walking up and down Tangier streets, I thought I saw the bald ghost of Ahmed Yacoubi, but he did not recognize me. Perhaps he was looking for his old landlord, the one who sold everything in his house when he was living in New York – the paintings and the furniture. As Yacoubi lay dying in America at the Cabrini Hospital, even then he was pursuing his landlord through a maze of dreams. The smell of cloves and oranges pervades my memory.

Oliver stands under a street sign looking at his map of Tangier. He remembers his first trip to Tangier. Paul offers him some M&Ms in a bowl (the peanut variety). Oliver refuses, afraid they may contain hashish, not realizing that if indeed they were *majoun* candies, he would no longer need to look for the real map of the city. But of course they were only M&Ms. Behind the veil is the reality. Only once does Scheherazade reveal the true tale. The nut is hidden within. Oliver's wife made a pillow for Paul with a batiked design containing the four-fingered hand of William Burroughs. I am not surprised if Paul doesn't sleep on it. Paul once suffered from photophobia, a painful aversion to light. He sleeps with a mask over his eyes and wax plugs in his ears. He once had two fleas in a tiny box. They were dressed in Mexican costumes, one male and one female. In 1970 we discovered that the female was gone from the little box within a box in a locked trunk. Now the mate has also mysteriously disappeared. Allah works in strange ways. We are only up to our second wish and already the genie is laughing on the mountaintop.

Brion's ashes scattered at Cap Spartel blew back in the faces of those who had assembled there – Anne, Paul, Targuisti, Hamri, Mme McBey, Udo and others. There is a rumour that they were not Brion's ashes at all but the remains of a chicken dinner consumed by the director of the Macadamia Foundation, Jima Khan himself. I am getting messages conducted through pink geraniums in my beard. The names of the streets have been obliterated, the records scattered to the wind. The last hustler chants a litany of old memories and lost lottery tickets. Philippe and Terry crash out as the ferry from Gibraltar pulls into the harbour. Still the number 1001 is barely visible on the door.

Genet liked to stay with Brion in his medina mahal. He liked Brion's joints and enjoyed insulting Hamri and arguing with him. He had a room in the Minzah, but was always getting into trouble for wandering around the hotel late at night in his pyjamas on Nembutal looking for a drink. Another toothless man passes my table. Tangier is an aquarium full of queer fish.

The schoolchildren are quiet this morning. Abdelouahaid said to Paul that there would be some kind of fiesta today, that the post office would be closed. I don't think Paul really wants the sleeping medicine refused to his doctor by the Moroccan pharmacy. If someone offers to get it for him, he changes the subject or brings up legal reasons against it, acts as if he has no choice in the matter. It is as if the door has been locked shut and only Moulay Abdullah has the key. Naturally he cannot go out unless it is permitted. Still, he is allowed visitors and his meals are served punctually. Gertrude Stein thought he was sensible in summer. Paul says he was never sensible. We laugh together like two conspirators.

Krazy Kat comes by with a note from Phillip Ramey about dinner on Tuesday. He says Paul named him Krazy Kat because he is a *non sequitur*, always changing from one subject to another. Krazy Kat is forty, though he looks younger, is still going to school for TV and media training. In Tangier he specializes in beach and gym. He has known Phillip for eighteen years. Phillip is suave with a good sense of humour. He mimics Virgil Thomson and others perfectly, takes on their physical personae completely when he says for example: 'He doesn't spurt, he just dribbles.' Phillip uses a cigarette-holder well and looks good pinned against a wall. He has a penthouse on 100th Street in Manhattan and writes programme notes for the Philharmonic, composes music he describes as dissonant. Even after fifty years Paul claims not to know where to buy ham in Tangier. When Phillip brings back a can of Danish ham, Paul is delighted and even sits up in a chair for a plate of ham and eggs. Paul has had a relapse of the sciatica after a few days of respite and is again bent over like a pretzel standing in at about three and a half feet. He allows himself only one kif cigarette per day.

I'm sitting in Number 43 around the corner from Dar Baroud. Mohammed has gone to get the two rabitas – little bouquets of grass. Now they are here, fresh and beautifully chopped. It all sticks together under the pressure of my thumb and the fragrance is delightful. No wonder Guerlain once made a perfume from kif called *Dawamesc*. Paul once had it in his perfume collection.

A French fag with dyed blond hair checks in at the hotel desk, looks at me and virtually creams with delight saying: 'Are you Paul

Bowles?' He is part of another camera crew come to interview Paul. He somehow thinks I am Paul and that I am waiting to greet him on his arrival. I am wearing my black gandoura with gold trim. In retrospect I'm more surprised that he doesn't expect me to carry his bags to his room. When the TV crew come to film Paul, he is looking for *The Sheltering Sky* book contracts. We talk of Duke Ellington, his aristocratic intelligence. Paul is on his back for the interview, says he doesn't really mind. 'It brings the money in,' he says. Mrabet, in the kitchen, is answering questions from the director. 'The first time I saw Paul he was walking with William Burroughs and Jane. . . .' No one seems to know that Sherifa is dead, only Targuisti. I see a photo of Jane with Sherifa veiled and wearing sunglasses.

We go to the opening of the Paul Bowles Colloquium at the newly named Samuel Beckett Theatre. It is a French cultural affair to honour Paul before his forthcoming eightieth birthday. The panel begins by addressing the question of whether or not kif is necessary for Paul's writing. The emphasis is placed on the fact that Paul, not surprisingly, answered once when asked that he could write without kif as well. At least there were no accompanying pictures of fried eggs sizzling in the pan. Terry bolted for the door, Raphael and I not far behind. We grab a petit taxi and head for Paul's, his presence being worth all the French-fried words about him and his work. Raphael and Paul get into a conversation about blood. Paul doesn't like the taste of his own blood, he says. I forget to ask him if he prefers the blood of others. Ralph Nelson and Mitsuko are there from Majorca and have been feeding Paul sushi. Michael Wolfe (Tomboctou Press) is also there. We all leave together when the Moroccan masseur comes to give Paul a massage.

Paul is in a good mood, very mellow. He says it's because of the pain. Paul agrees that Brion was mad and smiles sweetly. He seems puzzled when I tell him Brion said 'Not mad, only bad'. Then he smiles again as he gets it. Yes, Brion was a Master of Mischief. We talk about Alfred ('He was crazy'), Norman ('If I don't get what I want I can be very dangerous'), Irving ('He was awful, said he'd come to Morocco to teach me how to write and that Jane had defiled the Temple'). Only Irving had no excuse. I take many photos, including some of everyone sitting on Paul's bed. Paul didn't know Sherifa was dead. Said he was sorry. Then he said: 'Well, not that sorry.' Sherifa's temper was well known. She could have played the Wicked Witch of the West without any make-up. Mrabet makes Raphael a pipe and we discuss coming to visit him at his house.

Soon David Herbert's driver will come to pick us up – Noureddine, I think his name is. David thinks it was only fifteen years ago that we met, but it was closer to thirty years. Neither of us really remembers much about any meeting, but we look forward to today. This is my first invitation. The past rises to kiss the present. We will be outside in the garden and there will be caged birds everywhere. Two days before, Phillip found me and Raphael having coffee and almond pastries across from the Café Brasil on the corner of Holland and Mexico. David had sent him to make sure we had received his note. Phillip says not to miss the Van Dyck over the fireplace when a mad Moroccan suddenly appears in the street just in front of us and takes off his pants. He makes a few faces, runs distractedly this way and that, then sits on a car and puts his clothes back on while making more painful grimaces. Then as quickly as he appeared, he is off running down towards the Boulevard. All this without provoking more than a superficial response from the onlookers who take it in their stride with not much more than a glance or a shrug as if to say: 'It's all part of Allah's play.' Perhaps what he did was enough to cure him, but I doubt it. I take a clandestine photo, though I am aware that it is a dangerous act and Phillip tells me how once in the Socco he pulled Cherie Nutting away from a knife fight she was trying to photograph.

Paul tells me that, as an essential ingredient in the making of *majoun*, Yacoubi always included one drop of blood. Naturally I assume this is a drop of blood from the maker of the *majoun*. This is the magic of making something, the part of the maker without which the thing made will never be a true creation or have the fuerza. So in the Japanese story told by Lafcadio Hearn, the maker of the perfect bowl must finally become part of that bowl. Only by leaping into the molten mixture can the maker give the bowl the desired tone, the ultimate patina.

When I took the photos of Paul and Raphael, Paul gave all, holding on as if for life itself. Mrabet remembers coming to my house in Dar Baroud in 1965 to a great Jilala party. It was the night Farato drank the kettle of boiling water, the night M'sikseff poured the perfect tea, the night I danced like a drunken glider. I had just returned from the shrine of Sidi Heddi where I met the Bouhalla. In a dream Sidi Heddi, kif saint of Morocco, had come to me and told me to bring a kilo of the best kif to his place in Beni Aros on the Mehasen River, where I lost my pipe. . . .

It is dawn. I cannot sleep. Paul, though he wears ear-plugs, must have his noise machine on when he sleeps, a whirring propeller which makes a buzzing sound like an angry refrigerator. He can sleep only if he hears this sound through the ear-plugs. Only this way can he prevent himself from hearing that which he can't abide, the barking of a dog or the voices of his neighbours. Abdelouahaid fixes the noise machine and Paul smiles as happily as he does when Abdelouahaid or Mrabet call him 'Loco'. He is happy to be called mad by these men who take care of him. Who is not mad, after all? And love, of which no one speaks, is that not the greatest madness of all?

It was Phillip Ramey who held Samuel Barber's hand when he lay dying; it was Phillip who thought hard colon and listened to Virgil Thomson's antic raps. 'Well, it's all about who does what to whom and who gets paid.' He knows the importance of the precise note, doesn't care much for background music. Krazy Kat is tired and has to get back to Itesa, where they are staying in Jane's old apartment, now technically Buffie Johnson's place. They have only one key. Krazy Kat has a twin brother who calls him every three days from America. He knows someone wherever he goes.

Noureddine came in his white jacket and black tie to drive us to David Herbert's for lunch, already dressed to serve the meal. David is now eighty-three and not yet dotty, he says with a warm smile. 'It's nice to have your own heart back,' he says. Gavin Young, ex-foreign correspondent and expert on the marsh Arabs, a protégé of Thesiger, is also there. He is renting a villa nearby. David shows us the cover proof of his new book, *Engaging Eccentrics*, and the photos. I look at the one of himself and Cecil Beaton in drag for a play they were once in together.

'Poor Brion', 'Poor Paul', David likes to say. 'Jane was such fun, so witty.' The portrait of the Countess of Pembroke by Van Dyck is, as expected, over the fireplace. There are many framed pictures of beautiful women, Tallulah, Valentina Schlee, others all dead by now, all from drawings by David himself. Noureddine serves cottage pie. Terry and David discuss whether it can be made with beef or lamb. I forget to ask where the peacocks are, but it hardly matters. Whenever I think of David Herbert, I see in my mind's eye a muster of peacocks. 'Come again before I'm dead, will you? It's been such a pleasure.'

After lunch with David I see imaginary perukes on all the Nasranis, from David himself to Gavin and Paul; suddenly it seems as if we are all taking part in an eighteenth-century drawing-room comedy. The melons brought from Marrakesh were sweet and delicious. I take some photos and David obliges with a parrot or two. The view of Tangier from the mountain is grand. David tells a story of Jane being sick. Jane was saying that she might die and she asked David to find Sherifa, who then still wore her big straw hat and was selling grain in the market. He told Sherifa that Jane wanted her to come, to lie down next to her and that she would give her a radio. Sherifa waited and thought about it, then said: 'Tell Jane I want a taxi.' David says that Paul was Jane's life, that she had to find Sherifa to balance Paul's relationship with Yacoubi, that Sherifa only 'touched' Jane seven times in all those years. 'Poor Jane'.

The green colour of David Herbert's sitting-room was very bright, like the one green eye of a sheep I saw slaughtered years ago in Sidi Kacem. 'Daring', Gavin called it. Gavin is doing a book on all the places Joseph Conrad wrote about, the seaports of Indonesia and so on. When Gavin worked in Rabat, he sometimes came up to Tangier, where he would meet Ian Fleming at Dean's Bar. Fleming usually drank triple vodkas in a large glass with tonic and lemon. Gavin described him as a cad and a shit, but obviously respected him nevertheless. 'Now that my heart is my own again, I can give it to my friends.'

Martial music from behind the Socco Grande mixes with the call to prayer which begins to take over for a brief time and then gives way to chirping birds, trumpets and trombones, car horns and the incessant babble of people talking at dusk. Red Moorish doorways appear like mouths on the pages of Philippe's sketch-book as the brush attacks the paper of its own volition. Terry smokes a cigarette in flares of yellow and red at the end of a roll of colour film recovered from the dark-room. I was not sure if the large embroidered cloths and banners had inscribed on them the word ALLAH, or was it Coca-Cola? Phillip, who also doesn't read Arabic, says that he recognizes Coca-Cola in Arabic because it looks like YESS. Allah, too, is YESS as in affirmation, acceptance. Shebli flaps his arms under a tree, calling out, 'Who! Who!' Not a question, but a statement. It is He.

The Café Central decided to remodel, to modernize. They got rid of the old wrought-iron windows, got hideous new brown tiles for the outside and painted the inside so that it looks more like a hospital than a café. Bertolucci couldn't film there, so he found another café in the street with the two movie theatres leading up to the Casbah. Then he brought a train in, since there was a train going by the café, as described in Paul's book. ACCION EMOCION COLOR.

Mrabet doesn't waste any gestures and, although he serves, he was not made for serving. He is planning a big book, the Book of the True – where Janie will sit beautifully and sadly with her hand under her chin in front of an empty swimming-pool. I guess Paul must have his plum, Mrabet must have his cows and Jane the empty pool. Who knows what Mrabet speaks to the machine when all are sleeping, when he sits in his house and finally puts his pipe down? He knows how to wait and to watch. He knows how to keep something of himself in reserve. Raphael and I go with him to his house in Suani after he serves Paul his meagre plate of ham and lettuce leaves, his pastry. Paul didn't care much for the Prokofiev and he never liked Beethoven, although the thought of Bach's Offering brings a smile to his dry lips. We go to Mrabet's because I want to see him away from Paul just once in all these years. He has a few paintings and drawings, some little things of Brion's, a bleak landscape with two grey hills, between which one could only expect ambush, and a calligraphical birthday greeting full of 55s for Paul on his fifty-fifth birthday. That was 1965. Mrabet shows us his photo albums and I take some shots of him as he explains to Raphael, who turns the pages. . . . Mrabet before he was Mrabet, Mrabet the body-builder and acrobat walking on his hands through the sixties, smiling with Paul, who usually looks as if he has just been flustered by an uninvited guest, through the seventies. The pictures of Paul alone are portraits of the writer's profile, thinking or gazing inwardly. Then the eighties, with Paul often in bed, Mrabet popping out his false teeth in a parody of the sinister. Alfred banged on the door and screamed: 'Paul, Paul, Mrabet is going to kill me!' 'Sherifa never poisoned Jane,' Mrabet says. 'She was just a monkey.'

Mrabet sits in a cloud of smoke. I wonder if he thinks he smoked these strangers into existence. How did they get into his life, with his cows, his family, his house? His father, a long-time head pastry chef at the Minzah, what would he have made of these Nasranis with pointed teeth and blonde wigs, with their upside-down eyes and suitcases full of expensive dust?

Mrabet's wife and daughter set the table, and the three of us, Mrabet, Raphael and I, sit down to a feast. Mrabet, like Raphael, never takes carbonated drinks. He has about him a quality of olives and cooked lemons. I think he was right to argue with Yevtushenko. Even if he was wrong, he was right. Mrabet has won the lottery and almost lost his life. He knows how much to feed Paul for breakfast and how much ten cows eat in a week. He doesn't think Paul will ever die. He stands apart. He smokes alone. Whatever he promised Janie, whatever he never promised Paul, what it was he promised himself, back then in the beginning at Merkala – as a fisherman he knows that all you can do is cast your line and wait to see what appears from the deep.

I first met Mr Bowles in Tangier in 1960 – I love the past dead wonders of human life like Cézanne, Shelley, Pythagoras, Apollonius of Tyana, etc., like-kind. In my time no such wonderment of humankind have I encountered during many a sojourn.

But there were some – say, two? Burroughs, and Paul. Paul was the classiest, the sharpest, as well as redolent of science. I so wished to emulate him. But-me too New York City wild hot sweetheart plus pain in the neck. Decked in white suit, he carried lightly the whole Romantic age in his graceful stroll. Had I yearned to talk to Vermeer, Paul would fit the bill for me – and his wife, no sharper, true-spirited soul was ever enjoined.

How different my life had I accepted his invite to share home in Tangier. The Beauty of the old world is his to relay. I love him.

Fatefully his,
I am,
Gregory Corso

Anne Cumming

A Reticent Man

The first time I met Paul Bowles he was nesting like a bird on top of the sea wall of Asilah, a little fishing village on the Atlantic coast of Morocco. His apartment was actually *in* the wall, hanging over the beach. It seemed a suitable abode for this shy, birdlike man who often tucks his head under his wing and communicates only in writing.

I had been taken to see Paul by the Moroccan painter, Hamri, who pushed me through the door with the words 'You two should know each other', and then left us alone together. That was thirty years ago and I don't feel I know Paul yet. Does anyone? He is a reticent man.

I do not remember any of our conversation at that first meeting. I remember that we went down to the beach to take a walk. Arab fishermen, their pantaloons rolled up above bare brown legs, were wading into the sea to pull up their nets newly dragged in by small rowing-boats. Paul and I helped haul in the catch and bought some little fish from the still struggling mass which flopped around on the sand. Tiny crabs scuttled around, trying to escape back to the sea. A few small octopuses waved their tentacles. It was not a big catch, just the stuff of which fish soup is made.

We took our parcel of fish back to the apartment on top of the wall and laid it on the rough kitchen table. Then Paul made me a glass of mint tea, pouring it back and forth Moroccan style so the sugar mixed in well with the mint and the black tea. This little tea ceremony, usually done by a man, cemented our vague friendship.

I had seen Paul and his wife Jane on my previous visits to Tangier in the 1950s, in Dean's Bar or the Café de Paris. I had heard a lot of gossip about their unusual relationship. They lived in separate apartments, had same-sex lovers, but were cemented by a marriage that neither wished to dissolve. They never discussed the situation themselves, it was just there, accepted by themselves and their friends.

Paul's own autobiography *Without Stopping* is a beautifully written travelogue, but it does not tell us much about the man himself. He widens our horizons without taking us into his own inner sanctum. Although he has parted the bead curtains and let us view the mysterious Mahgreb, he has never let us into his own heart and soul. He is the least charismatic and most unrevealing cult figure I know. As narrator in the film of his book *The Sheltering Sky* he is almost invisible and partly inaudible. It is in his writing that he has come across to us. He writes because he does not talk much, and that is perhaps his strength. He is an observer, not a participator. He encourages us, his readers, to go out and get the experience. He set me off down desert paths of my own, and I do not regret a single grain of sand.

Charisma is difficult to define. On one level it is animal magnetism and energy – and Paul does not have that. On another level it is an aura of knowledge, life experience and quiet self-confidence. That he has, and this has made him a central figure in the literary world of our time. It has made other writers seek him out.

During the 'psychedelic summer' of 1961 when the entire Beat generation of writers rampaged through Tangier, trying every known drug and eating bat stew, Paul remained a quiet cult figure at its centre. He was there but not there. Janie hid. She was sure this outrageous invasion would ruin their private stamping-ground. But everyone got bored and moved on, leaving Paul in control of Tangier again. He was a cutural link between the Muslim world and the West, now living quietly in a modern building without a telephone but with an Arab companion. Journalists and friends continued to consult him. Publishers came and went, more books got written or translated from the Arabic, Janie became ill and died, Paul himself got ill but did not die. He is a quiet survivor. I met him occasionally during the seventies and eighties, but still never really got to know him. Our last encounter was in January 1987.

Paul's friend, and my adopted brother, Brion Gysin, had died in July 1986 in Paris. He had asked me shortly before his death to scatter his ashes at Cap Spartel, the rocky promontory near Tangier which had once been the Gardens of Hesperides where Hercules picked the golden apples in order to return to Olympus. This most westerly portion of Mediterranean Africa was conquered by Arab crusaders in the seventh century, and until Christopher Columbus discovered America it was considered the Edge of the World. The place is still a wild last outpost.

We had chosen what would have been Brion's birthday, 19 January. Paul and a few other close friends came with me. He was elderly but sprightly, having survived yet another illness. He hopped across the rough ground to the cliff edge above the Caves of Hercules where the Arab crusader Oqba Ibn Nafil rode his horse into the sea to show that there was no more land for Islam to conquer.

I gave everyone a handful of Brion's ashes, brought all the way from Père Lachaise in Paris. I suggested we all say a prayer or a poem, depending on our beliefs. We spread out, communing with ourselves and the departed. Paul had shown no emotion as I tearfully handed him a fistful of ashes. He was steeped in the Arab philosophy of Mektoub ('it is written'), where death is a part of life. He knew that Brion's soul would live on in his painting and writing, which would survive for ever, like his own, if that was the Will of Allah. Paul accepted the inevitable with ease, as was the custom of his adopted country. He stood frail but calm with his handful of ashes, his white hair blowing in the breeze as the sun miraculously came out above the wet fields blooming with early asphodels and wild iris. As he threw his ashes, some blew back in his face and he smiled, as if welcoming a last contact with his friend.

Millicent Dillon

Meeting Paul

In March 1977, as I was beginning work on my biography of Jane Bowles, I arrived in Tangier to meet Paul. I had had a pleasant but formal correspondence with him. I had, of course, read his work with its dark over- and undertones. I knew that Jane had called him 'Gloompot'. I suppose I expected someone formal and rather dour, perhaps even dark in his daily aspect.

To my amazement I found him, at that first meeting, to be witty, elegant, considerate and charming, with a certain easy detachment in that charm. He was, in fact, great fun to be with. I often thought of that discrepancy between what I anticipated he would be and how he appeared to me when I met him. Now and then I thought of that line of Mrs Copperfield in Jane's *Two Serious Ladies*: 'It is not for fun that I do this but because it is necessary to do so.'

On that first visit of six weeks my routine was unvarying. An early riser, I worked on my notes and questions in the morning. In the mid-afternoon Paul, who was a late riser, would come by the hotel in his car, driven by Abdelouahaid Boulaich, and then we would go to Paul's apartment in the Immeuble Itesa. After tea and conversation with visitors – there were always visitors – Paul and I would talk, often for four or five hours, of Jane and her work. Our conversation ranged widely, over Jane's life, over his and Jane's life together and apart. His willingness to be of help to me was unlimited. There was never, I felt, any evasion on his part, which was all the more astonishing considering how the darkness of her death lingered with him. I had brought with me information I had unearthed about her early and later life that he did not know. I had brought, as well, copies of sections of her unpublished manuscripts which were in the archive at the Humanities Research Center in Austin, Texas. Although these manuscripts were previously thought to be in a chaotic jumble, I had found them to have their

41

own specific order.

I was eager and excited, full of ideas and theories. Paul didn't hold much for theories about behaviour and over those weeks and my subsequent two visits to Tangier I came to learn a lot from him about the limits of theory in the knowing about others. I had never met Jane. She had died four years before, in May 1973, just as I came upon her work. Though she was my subject, Paul was the transmitter. He had the capacity to be present forcefully in his own being and yet to be the transmitter in a remarkably patient way.

I saw much other evidence of this patience in him with others too. Though Paul had an established literary reputation at the time, he was in the world's terms, if not neglected, certainly not famous. Still, unannounced visitors came in an unending stream to his apartment, brought by admiration and curiosity about him and his work. In the years since 1977, as he has become a legendary figure, that stream has turned into a flood, and the sheer number of visitors can no longer be reasonably accommodated. But then, as I remember, he turned no one away. Young writers came to him, seeking advice or simply conversation. Readers, young and old, who were caught up in his subject-matter and style, appeared. Others came for obscure reasons, as if they were seeking in him a monument, matching something in their own psyches. Still others came with demands, not clearly articulated. No matter how serious or how flaky, the visitor was welcomed with tea and attention and conversation.

In his autobiography and in interviews Paul has always taken the stance of someone abstracted from others, not deeply connected to others, yet as I observed it, there he was unfailingly courteous, giving of his time with apparently little thought of return. Was each person equivalent to every other for him? No, I don't think so. I think his acceptance of others, as they came to him, had something to do with some profound choice in him not to judge, allied to his belief that ultimately no one is knowable. Yet at the same time as he adhered to this ethical vision – for it was an ethical and moral choice on his part, I believe – he accepted the imposition upon himself of stringent external and formal rules of behaviour that arose from an earlier time in his life, from his parents' teachings, perhaps.

Virginia Sorensen Waugh once said to me, 'Paul's a saint', and I knew at once what she meant. Not a saint in ordinary terms – if one can use the word 'ordinary' about saints – but saintly in his adherence to his own vision of judgement and morality. In Paul's writing I detect the same combination of ethical choices, the refusal to judge his characters and the acceptance of the imposition of formality – and form – as binding upon him (which is perhaps another way of accepting Fate).

But I see I have fallen again into my old habit of theorizing. What I wanted to say about meeting Paul was simply this: out of my experience as the writer of the biography of Jane, I came to feel about Paul that he was a figure distant yet close, mysterious yet open, and above all, endearing. Now that I have not seen him for twelve years, it would be the greatest pleasure to go to the Immeuble Itesa, to go up that creaking, tiny elevator, to get out on the fourth floor, to knock on the door, to see it open and to see him before me. In my mind's eye, I can do it. His effect lingers.

Ruth Fainlight

A Memoir of Tangier and Paul Bowles

The fact that Paul Bowles lived in Tangier was one reason to accept an invitation from friends who had moved there. They did not know him, but arranged some sort of social event so that a meeting could take place. Paul and Alan, Jane and I – the four of us felt at ease together and admired each other's work. Learning that we had decided to stay for a while, the Bowleses suggested we might rent an apartment in their building.

The fact that we were neighbours gave a domestic tinge to the friendship. There were two sizes of apartments in the Immeuble Itesa: three-roomed ones like those which we and Jane (and her entourage) occupied, and smaller *garçonnières*, one of which was Paul's. His birds, though, lived on the terrace of the larger apartment, where much daily activity centred upon buying ingredients for and cooking the evening meal, every detail of which was related to his preferences. I never ceased to be intrigued and touched by this aspect of Jane and Paul's marriage, in which she was as dutiful and devoted as the most exemplary wife in an eighteenth-century manual, and he as correct and considerate as the model husband in a nineteenth-century one.

That first stay lasted about four months. By the time we returned, Tangier had been incorporated into the Kingdom of Morocco and I had given birth to our son David, who was then about eight weeks old. We'd kept in contact, and so the Bowleses knew that we wanted somewhere larger than the old apartment.

Paul wrote that he would book a room for us at the Hotel Atlas, where his friends usually stayed. It had not occurred to him that there were none of the facilities a mother and baby might need. When Jane arrived to inspect David and vet Paul's arrangements, I could tell she understood this, not only from sidelong glances of amusement but because she insisted we come to the apartment to eat with them every evening until we found a house.

Other dinner guests were Tennessee Williams and his friend Frank, who were in Tangier then. The men would lounge on low-cushioned seats along the wall, Moroccan style, smoking and talking, while Jane called out orders to Sherifa and the maid, who answered just as loudly as they moved in and out of the kitchen, and I concentrated on the baby and watched them all. Paul was recording Berber and tribal music for the Library of Congress, travelling far south beyond the Anti-Atlas Mountains, and sometimes showed us photographs of the tall mud casbahs of the region and played us extracts from his tapes. I remember an evening when Tennessee held David on his lap for ten or fifteen minutes. Each of them, adult and baby, stared deeply into the other's eyes, equally fascinated.

Paul's introduction to Marguerite McBey, a long-time American resident with a small house to rent in the grounds of her own on the Old Mountain, solved our accommodation problem. The house was furnished with fine Moroccan pieces and carpets, and stood in a large garden overlooking the Strait of Gibraltar. If visibility was good, it was possible to make out the town of Tarifa on the Spanish coast, thirteen miles away.

Once we had moved I saw less of Paul, unless he happened to be in Jane's apartment during one of my visits. These were very much female affairs apart from David, who lay in the centre of Jane's bed kicking his legs, the focus of much attention. Paul mentioned, one such afternoon, that in a few days there would be a festival at the shrine of a Berber saint, further down the coast, and asked if we would like to go with him and a few other friends.

Of the four men in the large car that came to collect us after dinner, Paul was the only one in Moroccan dress: a beautiful camel-hair djellaba. With his shorn blond head, pale eyes and lean, New England features, he looked the classical northern explorer.

The road was becoming a track and in the beam of the headlights I could see clouds of dust raised by our wheels. We had arrived – exactly where, I couldn't tell in the dark; only that we had stepped out of the car into a crowd of hundreds, even perhaps thousands, of men in white robes. Further off were small fires surrounded by groups of people, along with cafés and tea-houses, divided by barriers of thorn twigs or hurdles with carpets thrown over them. We sat down and Paul leaned across the little round wooden table that had been brought with the glasses of tea and told me to watch the dancer who approached, attracted by the presence of foreigners. At such close quarters, the broad young face, dripping with sweat, was more boyish than feminine. Under the shiny, gold-braided robe and heavy rows of charms and beads that hung from throat to waist, a supple body swayed and undulated. Those watchful eyes ringed with kohl soon decided there were better prospects elsewhere, because a few vigorous twirls of skirt and stamps of ankleted feet carried the dancer to another table, where the men were more openly appreciative. They began to compete with each other in pressing large dirham notes on to his wet forehead, which he peeled off and slid into the neck of the robe while smiling enticingly at the next potential donor. But it was all quite decorous, and as we walked through what I now saw was a temporary encampment of several thousand people (among whom we seemed to be the only 'Nasrani'), occupying a wide level area behind the Atlantic dunes south of Larache, I noticed how many armed soldiers mingled with the crowd.

A throbbing rhythm compelled me towards it. Ranks of white-robed men parted with almost magical ease to let me into the front row. I was surrounded by a delicious smell of wood-smoke, clean cotton cloth and the freshly washed bodies of people nourished on highly spiced food – every one of whom was enthralled by the drumming and high-pitched, repetitive chanting of the players. I felt completely safe and forgot about the others. But they had kept an eye on me, and eventually Alan came to lead me away to a café for another glass of tea.

Paul was amused by my 'boldness', and commented that before the government had begun official supervision by the military and the police, the behaviour of the Aïssaoui, and members of other ecstatic sects, had been very different. A few years later, I found the following description in Murray's *Handbook to the Mediterranean* of 1890:

The fanatic religious dances of the Aïssaoui occasionally take place in the native quarters of the town. These performances commence with the beating of drums and tambours, after an interval of which, one of the Aïssaoui, being inspired, rushes with a yell into the ring formed by the spectators, and begins a frantic dance, the body being swayed backwards and forwards, and contorted with fearful violence. He is soon joined by others, who continue their maniacal gestures and cries until they fall exhausted, or are stopped by the Mokkadam (head of the order). The next proceeding consists of forcing out the eyes with iron spikes, searing themselves with red-hot iron, eating live scorpions and serpents, chewing broken glass and the leaves of the prickly pear, etc., all of which acts seem to be performed under the influence of fanatical mania, the performers being apparently insensible to pain. The sight is well worth seeing *once* for those who have tolerably strong nerves, but few persons would care about witnessing an Aïssaoui fete a second time.

The sky was absolutely clear, full of stars, and the moon was full. It was midsummer eve, and Sidi Kacem's holy well and sacred tree, whose branches were always swathed with rags and strips of cloth tied on by women anxious to become pregnant and men who wanted riches or revenge, must have been a site of worship long before the arrival of Islam. We were walking through an area of tents, softly lit by oil lamps or candles. A murmur of voices came through the thin cloth walls, and shadows played across them as those inside moved around. At last I found where the women and children were. With the approach of dawn, the sky overhead seemed even darker, as if the night were concentrating into a smaller area, but at the horizon a pure turquoise light began to surge upwards.

We had all met again without making any attempt to do so, and seemed to be part of an increasing movement eastwards, towards the crest of the furthest dunes. By the time we reached it, the sky reflected every pale nacrous colour of the beach that stretched below us towards the line of surf several hundred metres away, and south and north as far as the eye could see or the imagination encompass. The scale was immense: we looked from Africa to America. Men in white and pale-toned robes streamed by, hurrying down the slope to the shore, diminishing in size with astonishing rapidity. Everything was tawny, like the pelt of an enormous lion. Some of the younger men were stripping off their robes as they reached the edge of the sea and strode into the shallow waves. Horsemen plunged past us, sending up a spatter of grainy sand as they dislodged clumps of tough sea-grass. A pale grey and then a white horse galloped close together at the water's edge, splashing their naked riders with foam. I felt as if I were viewing an immense painting, or even had become part of one. I looked at Paul. For a moment I was convinced that I saw it through his eyes: the realized ideal of Morocco.

Having had the distinct honour of being one of Paul Bowles's minor publishers for many years, I want to add my voice to the chorus of *Yeas!* and *Ayes!* for his eighty-second year on earth!!!

lawrence ferlinghetti

Charles Henri Ford

Five Haiku for Paul Frederic Bowles
('Freddie' to Gertrude Stein)

i

You make fantastic
Art out of their
Realistic depictions

ii

Ghost in the mirror
That grain of melancholy
Blooms or it busted

iii

Surprising himself
Is half the satisfaction
He derives from art

iv

For reasons which he
Cannot fathom he opens
Poetry's locked door

v

Where he wanted to
Be when he wanted to be
A life's achievement.

David Herbert

From Second Son

I still cherish an affection for the Villa Mektoub, because it was here that my friendship began with Paul Bowles and his wife Janie. They were staying at the Hotel el Fahar with Truman Capote and his friend Jack Dunphy. Jack had already published several novels but Truman's first book *Other Voices Other Rooms* had only just come out. It was acclaimed the book of the year and Truman, the young wonder of American literature, as a result of all this, had to cut his visit short and return to the States. Cecil Beaton also had to go back to London for business reasons and I was left alone at the villa.

As Janie and Paul were remaining in Tangier for a few more weeks I asked them to stay. We lived together for six weeks, sharing expenses. It was a memorable time for me and to be with them was an unending pleasure. Janie was small and dark with enormous brown eyes and a shock of dark curly hair; her nose was tiptilted and her mouth slightly negroid, and she resembled an unpredictable marmoset. Paul is tallish, fair with pale china-blue eyes and so delicately made that a breath of wind could blow him away. He has the beauty of a fallow deer. They had been married quite some time but their enjoyment of each other's company was undiminished. It was touching and extraordinary to hear them talking and laughing in the next room as though they had just met and were being at their most scintillating in order to charm each other. The Bowleses' marriage was based on mutual admiration and deep affection; nothing could spoil this ideal relationship.

Janie's mind, delivery of speech and timing were completely individual. She was unlike anyone else I have ever encountered. Her strange combination of comedy and tragedy were unique. Before you had time to laugh at some glorious sally, she had turned the joke into something so infinitely sad you were almost in tears. The same quality pervades her novel, *Two Serious Ladies*; her play,

In the Summer House; and her collection of short stories. I feel Janie is the one person I have met who may be said to have been 'touched by the finger of Genius'.

Paul's character is different. He is a fascinating person too and, though a very successful writer, is primarily a musician. He admits that it was reading Janie's *Two Serious Ladies* that started him on his own career as an author. His music is brilliant and original and his writing too is masterly, even if perhaps less individual than Janie's. His humour is subtle and unexpected because he always gives the impression of being intensely serious. He is very meticulous. I once had a headache and asked Janie if she had any aspirin. 'No, but look in Paul's medicine cabinet,' she said. I did, and took two. The following day Paul said: 'Janie, did you take two aspirins out of the bottle?' 'No, but David did.' 'Oh, that's all right. I just wondered because the last time I took one there were seventy-three left in the bottle and now there are only seventy-one.'

Paul is scared of any form of authority. He can even be nervous of a second-rate junior consular official for fear that he may be doing or is thought to have done something contrary to the policy of the United States Government. He is unable to get it into his head that on the whole such officials are there to get one out of trouble rather than into it.

He once befriended a young Moorish painter, Yacoubi, who became successful with exhibitions of his work in London and New York. Yacoubi got into some difficulties with the police and was arrested, though, as it turned out, there was no real case against him. However, the muddle was such that he languished in prison for several months. Though Paul had nothing to do with the affair, Yacoubi was his protégé and he sent food in to him and did everything he could to arrange for his release. Eventually we heard that the trial was imminent and it was rumoured that Paul would be called as a witness. He panicked at once and, with Janie, fled to Portugal. This proved unnecessary. The trial never took place; Yacoubi was freed and the whole episode forgotten. This terror of authority may stem from Paul's extreme youth when he was a member of the Communist Party at the time it was outlawed in the States.

Janie developed a passion for a Moorish woman from the grain market from whom she bought food for her parrot. She was a Sherifa and was always referred to as such. She sat, cross-legged, on a shelf in her booth wearing a *haik* and the large straw hat country-women wear, the crown and brim of which are joined by black cords that look like guy-wires. She had several gold teeth and a faint moustache; beneath the *haik* of white cotton protruded blue jeans and large brown golfing shoes. She never spoke to Janie but, in spite of this, Janie's infatuation for the Sherifa was such that she visited the booth three times a day and the parrot received three times its normal food.

At about this time Janie developed measles. Owing to her weak eyes the doctor insisted that she should remain in a darkened room. She was infinitely bored. One day she said to my Moorish servant, Addi: 'Please go to the grain market and ask the Sherifa if she will come and sleep on the floor of my bedroom during my illness. If she does, I will give her a radio!' The message came back: she would not come and sleep on the floor for a radio but she would consider it if Janie gave her a taxi and a chauffeur's uniform.

Janie recovered from measles and the great day came when the Sherifa consented to go on a picnic – but only if she could bring along her friend Kinzah. They arranged to meet in a public garden near the cattle market.

Janie prepared the food and took a taxi to the appointed place. She dismissed the taxi and sat waiting patiently on a bench for an hour and a half. Finally there appeared a large cream-coloured mule, on which were perched the Sherifa and Kinzah. The Sherifa was in front and Kinzah behind with a silver tray and teapot between them. They stopped and endless Arab politenesses ensued. Eventually the Sherifa asked Janie to hand up the picnic basket: no sooner was it in her hands than she whipped up the mule, which galloped off in a cloud of dust, leaving Janie disconsolate on the side of the road.

The courting and eventual winning of the Sherifa was an arduous task that took several years to accomplish. It is a great pity that this was ever achieved, as she turned out to be a wily woman who then dominated Janie completely.

The Bowleses bought a house in the Casbah. Only Janie could have found such a place – it was wider at the top than at the bottom and the front door might have been designed for an emaciated dwarf – by bending double you could just squeeze through it sideways. The door gave straight on to a perpendicular staircase, the first step of which could just hold one person. It gradually widened until you reached a small square landing. Off this, on one side, was a minute sitting-room with no window and, on the other side, a black hole which served as the kitchen. On you climbed, the stairs getting wider until you came to a large, almost palatial bedroom out of which ran another perpendicular staircase, which reached a vast terrace. One's legs ached from the ascent.

It was a particularly odd choice, as Janie had a stiff knee caused by tuberculosis of the bone when she was a child, and it was difficult enough for her to walk on a flat surface.

That first November, the Bowleses and I motored back to England, arriving in time for the publication of Paul's novel *The Sheltering Sky*. We spent a few days in Paris on the way and I telegraphed my housekeeper to prepare for us. Unfortunately the telegram never arrived and the house was empty and cold. Paul feels the cold infinitely more than most people and our arrival was spoiled. But from that time on we saw each other frequently and when I eventually emigrated to Morocco they became my constant companions.

In 1957, at the early age of thirty-nine, Janie had a stroke from which she never properly recovered. Her eyesight was affected and, being the sort of writer who must see the words on the page, she was unable to continue working. Although she gradually improved, the old Janie never quite reappeared. She was still amusing, original and subtle, but her inability to express herself as she wished, verbally or on paper, tried her sorely. Her genders, for example, became muddled and she used often to refer to the doctor, good-looking and exceptionally male, as 'she' in his presence. This could be disconcerting and certainly often made it difficult to carry on a normal conversation with her.

When Janie was well enough to be moved, she went first to a clinic in England and then to one in America. In both these hospitals she received shock treatment and she returned to Tangier in a much better state of health, which continued for several years. Later, alas, she started slowly to deteriorate, mentally and physically, until she became incapable of looking after herself. The doctors told Paul that there was nothing more to be done; the whole system was slowing down in the same way that it often does with old people after they have had a stroke. Janie had been so young when she had had hers that it had taken ten years for this process to begin.

Paul was distraught and unable to write, compose or accomplish anything. Janie had to be sent somewhere where she would be properly looked after. He heard of a Catholic nunnery near Malaga and, as Janie had always loved Spaniards, he sent her there.

Just at this time a collected edition of her works was published in one volume and had an enormous success. The notices were marvellous and, thinking to cheer her up, I made a collection of them and took it with me when I went to see her. As reading was such an effort, Janie made me read them to her. She looked very sad and for a little while said nothing, then, hopelessly, she said: 'I know you meant this kindly, darling, but you couldn't have done anything more cruel!' I was aghast. 'You see,' Janie went on, 'it all makes me realize what I was and what I have become.'

I was terribly upset. Janie, seeing this, looked up with a ghost of a smile. 'Give me the book,' she said. I handed her *The Collected Works*. With a trembling hand she picked up a pencil and added *of Dead Jane Bowles*. She had not quite lost her touch for mingling the absurd with the tragic.

We often used to visit her and sometimes were able to take her out for lunch or dinner. She seemed reasonably happy and slightly better and, in 1969, Paul decided to bring her home for a spell to see how things went. It was disastrous. Janie lay on the floor most of the day, staring at him. She would not eat and hardly spoke. There were still flashes of the old wit, but it was obvious she would have to return to the home. On her last evening I persuaded her, with great difficulty, to come out with me to dinner. She would only go to Guitta's Restaurant, where Mr Guitta and his daughter Mercedes had served her for many years, and where we could eat quietly in the garden.

Janie had taken great pains with her appearance as she knew how I loved her to look her best. Her hair was combed, her face made up and she was wearing her best black chiffon dress. By this time she could walk only with the help of two people, but she made a brave effort and we sat down to dinner. She was quite indifferent to what she ate.

'Would you like a shrimp cocktail, Janie?'

'What? Oh yes, if you like.'

'Would you then like lamb cutlets?'

'All right.'

'What sort of wine would you like, red or white?'

'Don't care.'

It was hard work but I talked away during the meal and at moments she responded. I was so happy to be with her again that I almost enjoyed myself.

'What a lovely evening we've had, Janie. Just like the old days.'

'Yes, wasn't it,' said Janie, 'except that I haven't opened my mouth once.'

'Anyway, you are much better and I'm going to give a party for you.'

'If you do, you'd better give it in the cemetery because I'm dead.'

I realized that there was no point in prolonging the agony, as Janie was leaving with Paul in the morning. We thought she did not know this as he had decided not to tell her in case she worried all night. I dropped Janie home and said: 'Good-night, darling. I'll ring you in the morning.'

'Do if you like,' she replied, 'but I shan't be here.' And she quietly closed the door. This was infinitely more upsetting than the vegetable silences.

After returning to Malaga, Janie wrote to Paul that she had embraced the Catholic faith 'to make it easier for you, dear Bubbles. They don't like burying Jews in Spain.'

Patricia Highsmith

A North African Encounter

Paul Bowles has his own way of doing things. It is hard to imagine a New Yorker falling in love with Tangier and choosing to spend most of his life there, in a city where the telephone (Paul's anyway) doesn't work because of inefficient repair jobs; in a building where the lift works when it wants to, and the concierge is said to be illiterate in any language; where the two dozen post-boxes on an inner wall downstairs have long ago been rendered useless by hammer or axe. Paul takes a walk twice a day, and on at least one of his walks picks up his post at the Socco. He is not the recluse that is rumoured. With regular and balanced meals and a glass of water as beverage, Paul is still going strong.

Perhaps it is the fatalism and the otherness of Morocco, depressing and dismaying to so many, that attracts Paul. One has the feeling that Paul Bowles sees life as it is: meaningless in the long run, sees humans as indifferent to suffering and death as is mother nature herself. Paul looks at this steadily, and tells it simply.*

August 1988

I went to Tangier for the first time. A friend had said to me: 'I hope you see Paul Bowles when you're there because Tangier without Paul wouldn't be Tangier.' Certainly it wouldn't for American writers, young writers from all over, who may not have an introduction, or may lack the audacity to ask where Paul lives, or the courage to knock, once they find out. Knock is what one must do, because he's cut his telephone off: the repair jobs were never adequate, and the telephone bills had to be paid anyway. 'Or

* It is the section following this preamble that originally appeared in *Vogue* in 1989.

you can't leave the country,' says Paul.

As it happened, my hostess was not in when I arrived, and Paul lives in the same five-storey building. Ringing her bell brought no response. 'You want *Paul* ——', said one of the two Moroccan women, dwellers in the building, who had accompanied me to my hostess's apartment door. They thought that I surely wanted Paul. All, such as I, want Paul. I knew him slightly from years back, when I lived in New York, and he knows my hostess. So I was admitted by a Moroccan who happened to be in Paul's apartment at the time, and Paul hospitably received me, even though he was having a solitary dinner then.

Tangier to me might well be Mars, Jupiter or the moon. The tempo of existence, as I was to learn in the next days, the connection with others – all this is different. As so it was odd that first evening, and later, to hear Paul speaking in more or less the same accent as mine, yet to realize that his existence is so different.

He has an efficient-looking tape-recorder in his bedroom, into which he records people speaking Arabic, and later translates it. In his entrance hall a stack of some ten old, dusty and perhaps nostalgic suitcases seems in slight danger of toppling. It's a darkish apartment, well curtained, full of personal atmosphere, shelves of books, as if he wants to draw within himself a concentration of his thoughts and experiences. This contrasts oddly with his openness to outsiders, rank strangers. He listens, he translates, he cares about them. He finds time for them. But he is perhaps more selective than I know. When I encounter him walking in the neighbourhood – as I did several times in the week I was there – he is always in the company of a young writer or two. It is as if these strangers, writers, young people gather round Paul, saying: 'Tell us about life, about your *life*. What does life mean? What does my life mean?'

Paul sees life with a reality and an honesty. He is open-eyed to human sadism, to merciless killing of man or beast by beast or man, open-minded to the meaninglessness of it all. Maybe that is why the young people and the not-so-young cluster round him, knocking on his door, slipping notes under it. 'Can we talk with you, Paul? Tell us the *truth*.'

Now back in the antipodes (Switzerland), where I live, I think of question after question I'd like to ask Paul, and shall by letter. He will have the patience to answer. He gives a lot to other people.

John Hopkins

Extracts from a Journal: Paul Bowles in Tangier

December 19 1962 – Tangier

Paul and Jane Bowles came to the Casbah today. Jane, frequently consulting her cracked mirror, at first seemed aloof, but during the meal, by her interest and intensity (caring, really), drew me further out of my shell than I have been in a long time. I found myself talking about my sister and the divorce and its effects on both of us – subjects I had thought of little interest to others.

Jane, when she said goodbye: 'There is no major or minor.'

March 31 1963

Dinner with the Bowleses in Jane's tiny apartment. They are married, but they share an affection and sense of fun as if they were brother and sister, not man and wife. There is an intimacy that seems not sexual but fraternal. They live in separate apartments one above the other, which are connected by a squeaking mauve toy telephone. Jane: 'Fluffy (squeak), come on up. Dinner (squeak) is ready (squeak).' Jane does the cooking. Tonight it's jugged hare in a red wine sauce. Delicious. Then there is the cat and the parrot. It's a bit like being in New York except for Sherifa, who rattles on in Arabic in her gruff, mannish voice, and laughs uproariously at her own jokes. A curiously alien presence who acts like she owns the place.

November 3 1963

Yesterday a photograph in the Casbah with Bill Burroughs, Paul and Jane Bowles, Joe McPhillips, Omar Pound, Christopher Wanklyn and Emilio Sanz, a Spanish writer. This is supposed to be literary Tangier. As Burroughs says: 'Tangier wins by default. If this were the 1930s, I'd be in Shanghai.' Paul: 'Tangier is out of the mainstream. It's a backwater. It has changed less than most places, or is changing more slowly.'

February 8 1964

Yesterday Paul told me that he is not interested in flesh-and-blood characters, but in people as embodiments of ideas. Rather like Camus. Situations and ideas, especially abstract ideas, interest him more than human beings.

April 5 1964 – Ain Sefra, Algeria

On Paul's recommendation we have come to this place where Isabelle Eberhardt drowned in a flash flood sixty years ago.

April 10 1964

Returned to Tangier to find a letter from Sonia Orwell at *Art and Literature* magazine in Lausanne. She has accepted my short story 'All I Wanted Was Company.' Eureka! All thanks to Paul. He read the story and suggested I send it in.

We run into Burroughs chez Bowles, eating *majoun*. Then we run into him again having dinner in the cellar at Paname's. He regales us with his Peruvian adventures, which have us shrieking with laughter. The *majoun* helps. Most nights he sits alone at the Parade having dinner at 7 p.m. even before the drinkers arrive. He likes to eat good food. Unlike most solitary diners, he doesn't bring a book or a newspaper. He just sits there alone, poker-faced, looking at the wall.

August 23 1964

Irving Rosenthal enters Paul's apartment, screams and cowers in the corner with his hands over his eyes.

'What's wrong?' Paul asks.

'That thing – what is it?'

'A parrot.'

'I've never seen one before! Take it away!'

Ira Cohen: 'I know he is guilty, but I am not sure of what.'

Norman Glass: filing a lawsuit against his mother 'for being a Jew.'

These are the kind of characters you run into in Paul's apartment.

August 25 1964

Paul has rented the Bonnet's cliff house on the Old Mountain for the summer. Last night Paul, Brion Gysin, Joe McPhillips and I watched Larbi Layachi [author of *A Life Full of Holes*, translated from the Arabic by Paul Bowles] make *majoun*. Larbi's recipe calls

60

for almonds and walnuts, wild honey from his father's apiary and a small mountain of chopped kif. We each get a peanut butter jarful. Later, stoned, we walk out to the cliff. A big moon hanging over the Straits leaves a slippery track across the water.

Brion: 'We're here to go.'

Paul: 'We're here to learn.'

December 6 1964

Paul's idea, having heard me talk about my raft trip down the Amazon, is to use the jungle river as a setting for a novel. A continual progression, change in scenery, time, thought, action. 'Boy, never underestimate the opposition.' W. Burroughs. His encounter with Protestant missionaries and their snot-nosed kids in Peru: 'Among them a man has to take a drink on the sly. They don't like to see a man take a drink.'

March 10 1965

Bowles talks of the African people in *Yallah*: 'How much . . . we could learn from them about man's relationship to the cosmos, about his conscious connection with his own soul . . . where we could learn *why*, we try to teach them the all-important *how*, so that they may become as rootless and futile and materialistic as we are.'

March 1 1967

One admires Brion and Paul and Bill because they have broken the mould.

March 7 1967

Wild children have taken over Calla Larache, where Bill Burroughs lives. 'Every day there seem to be more of them,' Brion says. '*Every day!*' It is difficult and even dangerous to visit Bill's house. The children grow angry if their games are interrupted. Paul thinks Bill eggs them on. He pays these kids to throw stones at strangers so he can get on with his writing.

May 19 1967

Brion in a gloomy mood: 'Man, I'm bordering on the great depression! I can't remember any more how human I am, or even if I am human. The simplest problem confounds me. I seem to have forgotten everything I ever knew. I have difficulty taking the easiest, most obvious steps, in making the most straightforward statements and decisions. I don't look forward to anything ... nothing!'

Paul on Brion: 'Drugs have altered his character. He has experimented too much.'

November 4 1967 – Marrakesh

Why does Paul live in Tangier? Because it is poised between the timeless civilization of the Mediterranean and the timeless nothingness of the Sahara. This kind of balance appeals to him.

February 13 1968 – Chelsea Hotel, NYC

Letter from P.B. in Tangier:

... You ask about my summer plans. At the moment there are none, although Jane's health could conceivably invent something by then, I suppose. I feel sure I shall be here or hereabouts. Who wants to be elsewhere? ... Really nothing happens in Tangier, or, at least, nothing that I am aware of.

Mrabet went yesterday to a saint's tomb somewhere near Ksar el Kebir, returning today in a happy state. He now believes the *tseuheur* which he suspected someone had made against him has been annulled, so we can rest in peace for a few days, maybe.

The weather has been clear and warm up until two days ago, when the clouds gathered in answer to rain-prayers that were being led by the *fquihs* all over town. It poured all night, and managed to flood the streets. There are still lakes here and there, and the frogs suddenly became very vocal under my windows. Unfortunately I can't record them, as all my tape-recorders are out of commission.

February 15 1968 – Hotel Chelsea, NYC

Letter from Brion Gysin in Tangier:

... The weather is beautiful but the town seems emptier every day.... Jane wasn't the only crazy who rang the bell or hammered at the bathroom window.... Mrabet got married last week but Paul doesn't know about that yet. Targuisti *dixit*. I can only tell you that January has been a jewel. I got some good recordings of 60 or more little kids praying for rain and it's like a summer day outside, right now.

April 1 1968

After dinner at Marguerite McBey's, Paul and I visit Alfred Chester in his house at the bottom of the Old Mountain Road. He looks like an enormous, hairless baby who must be treated like one to be happy. Otherwise he pouts. He has a pack of dogs that sleep in the same bed with him. The place stinks of dog piss. One room is shoulder deep with firewood, another with a mountain of oranges that look as though they have been delivered by a dump truck. There is a drunken fat woman with red hair. A Moroccan boy asks if we want tea or orange juice. Alfred starts taking off his clothes in front of the roaring fire. 'Why don't you stay?' he asks. 'Why are you going? Will you come back?' He calls the fat woman 'the living end'. He comes out into the wintery night with no clothes on. Fat blubbery hairless flesh. 'Of course you won't come back! You're snobs! You hate us! Just say so – will you come back?'

July 27 1968 – Malaga

A nun led me up the garden path to the main building. It was nearing lunch-time and all the ladies were sitting out on the front porch. They chattered to each other. My eyes went among them and picked out Jane sitting silent and alone on a bench in the back. The nun helped her to her feet. I kissed her, and she said: 'What are you doing here?' Two hours later I went away from that place. The life had been crushed out of her – by drugs and by disease. There is practically no spirit left. She said she felt she would never leave that place. One day could be no different from another. The nuns say she does not even wish to leave her room. She is ashamed of her shaggy appearance and asked me not to ask other friends in Tangier to visit her.

Letter from Mohammed Mrabet, dictated to Paul Bowles and translated from Arabic and typed by him:

> Casa Zugari, Calle Ajdir,
> Merstakhoche, Tanger, Maroc.
> 22/v/74
> Las once en punto.

Dear John,

I send you many greetings. Friend John: It's very hot in here. Last Monday I had a big dream about you. I was asleep, and I saw you dancing with the Jilala, dressed all in white. And you were working with fire in your hands. There were a lot of English and Americans watching, and even some Moroccans, and they were all astonished. And you went on dancing with this burning tree-trunk in your hands, and you rubbed it over your face. Finally, when you finished dancing, I went up to you and asked you how you felt. You said: I feel as though I had been born yesterday. This is the true life, the way it should be. I got up and began to dance with a long knife in my hand. And there was blood everywhere. Everyone was afraid. Afterward, when I had ended the dance, there was neither blood nor a sign of a scar. You came and asked me how I felt. I said I felt that I was in Heaven. Then we laughed a great deal and I woke up. Amigo Hopkins, heat always feels hot, but fire can always be put out. If not with water, with earth. If not with earth, with green plants. If not with green plants, with a hard look. Thoughts are not the same. There are many people who believe what others say. And there are many others who don't. Amigo John, I want to ask you some questions, those questions I spoke about with you some time ago, and which you said you would answer.

First question: Why do you prefer Morocco as a place to live in, to the United States?

Second question: You've spent more than ten years in Morocco, much of it in Tangier, and some of it in Marrakesh. According to you, what are the best things in Tangier and what are the least good? And the same about Marrakesh.

Third question: Can you tell me why you want to travel across the Sahara on a camel by yourself?

Amigo John, the fourth question: I've noticed that you like the Jilala and also that you love to dance. Can you explain why you like to enter into the music of the Jilala? How do you feel when you dance?

Amigo Hopkins, life is very sad, and the world is very happy. And the sky is weeping, and the earth is drinking, and the sea drowning. The rocks are dancing and the trees are singing. The roses are screaming and the birds are moving. Amigo John, Paul and I are going to Marrakesh to spend a few days with you in your house in the oasis. In the year

1811, as you well remember, we were in Russia together; this was when we had been captured as spies and were in prison. The worms crawled out of our noses in that jail, and we sold them to the Russian soldiers to make tortillas with. Amigo Hopkins, don't forget the time you ate the donkey's ear and found it delicious. Amigo John, drink lots of well water, and take showers with well water, and you must travel a great deal and eat plenty and have many pretty girls. That is the world – enjoy oneself because death is at one's heels. Youth disappears and sicknesses arrive, and pains, and one is always tired. Amigo John, many thanks and gracias. Si quieres. Si no quieres, gracias. Adios, hasta Dios quiere. Buena suerte. Hasta pronto.

Mohammed Mrabet

April 27 1975 – Marrakesh

Paul Bowles, he sits in that dingy apartment, his fur-lined foxhole, no telephone, yet he seems to know what's going on everywhere. You show him a book that has just arrived from NY; he's already read it. You can't wait to tell him some spicy bit of gossip you've just heard, but he already knows about it. How does he do it? What's his secret?

May 14 1978

Paul and I met Lilly Kalman's strange poet husband at her party. A prof. at Columbia. Dark, strange and emotional from so many years in the camps. After dinner back with Paul to his place for one K. cigarette and tea. He peppered me with literary questions, which meant he has begun reading *The Flight of the Pelican*.

June 13 1991

The high points of each day happen of 6 o'clock. At 6 a.m. we drive out to Cap Spartel to swim in the Atlantic and run on the beach; and each evening at 6 we go to Paul's to sit at the master's feet, to smoke the weed, and laugh.

Mrabet: 'Every year we get older, uglier and poorer, but look at Paul. Every *day* he gets younger, better looking and richer. What's his secret?'

Aeschylus in *Agamemnon*: 'To learn is to be young, however old.'

Buffie Johnson

Memoirs of Paul Bowles in the Forties

When Paul's autobiography, *Without Stopping*, was reviewed in *The New York Times*, it was given to the eminent composer, Virgil Thomson. As a friend of Paul's, I was dismayed to read that negative review. Since I had run into Paul at Virgil's, I had thought they were good friends, but I realize now that Aaron Copland was Paul's mentor and, perhaps, professional rivalry played a part in Virgil's criticism. When I next saw Virgil, I asked him why he had given it such a review. 'Well Bebe,' which was his pet name for me, 'Paul never *said* anything.' As William Burroughs said, it should have been called *Without Telling*. I had to admit to myself, in this book alone he gave a perfunctory outline of his life, studded with celebrated people and places, revealing nothing of himself. In it, Paul characteristically played down his personal life. The Italian director, Bertolucci, was astute to notice that Paul's life-role was that of a spectator, a cameo part in which he cast Paul for the film version of *The Sheltering Sky*.

Paul Bowles belonged to a clique consisting of some of the best creative talents in New York during the forties, a distinguished group of avant-garde. Once a month this group met at the house of Kirk Askew, the renowned art dealer. Although we all knew each other, his salon was somehow the cohesive centre. The criterion for this select company was certainly not publicity or beauty but solely talent. Once a year each member received an invitation from Kirk to attend his salon. This group included, among others, the artist/architect, Frederick Kiesler, known best for designing the underground building to house the Dead Sea Scrolls, as well as composers such as Virgil and Aaron Copland; and also figures like Phillip Johnson and Tennessee Williams. It was at Kiesler's penthouse that I first met Paul.

I visited Kiesler one day, and while he was showing me some of his extraordinary designs, the door to the guest-room opened and a handsome, young, impeccably dressed man emerged in light, semi-tropical clothes to match his blond hair. He set out to charm me and indeed his behaviour was charming in some contrast to his rather cool demeanour with strangers. I knew who he was, since I had recently become a friend of his wife, Jane. Before I left, Paul had succeeded in delighting me. My memory of that occassion remains fresh, for he gave me a gift of some solid, oriental perfume which he helped me to transfer to a little French, Victorian shoe I used for matches, so that every time I opened my purse, the odour would envelop me. This was early in his career when Paul was enjoying a considerable success as a composer through his theatre scores. After he wrote the music for Tennessee Williams's *The Glass Menagerie*, many of his other friends in the theatre also gave his commissions. He turned to writing when he began living in exotic places where there was no opportunity to hear his compositions played.

Paul translated Sartre's play, *Huis clos*, under the title *No Exit* for the New York stage. It was surprising that it was even produced because existentialism, though it was the excitement of the day, was not widely understood in America. This was certainly an 'in' production and Paul was the one who pulled it all together. Virgil called our group 'The Little Friends' and they filled all aspects of this production. Paul's cousin, Oliver Smith, produced the play, John Huston directed it and Kiesler designed the sets and costumes. Ruth Ford was the leading lady, while the supporting cast consisted of Anabella, the French actress, Claud Daphain and Pauline Potter, who became the Baronesse Guy de Rothschild. *No Exit* won an award for best foreign play.

For the last ten summers I have lived in Tangier in Jane's old apartment below Paul. I am welcome any time in his apartment, a pleasure he extends to intimate friends. He has no telephone to sort out the invited from the uninvited, so his living-room in the afternoon is an open house. Heaven knows when he has time for writing. He has written and still writes a great deal, but I have never caught him in the act. In the afternoon his salon is filled with pilgrims, some interesting and many, as he last wrote, ghastly.

In New York, the composer Phillip Ramey, the photographer Cherie Nutting, and her musician husband Bashir Attar and I talk continually about Paul, I think because Paul remains a mystery.

Paul never, never says how he feels. This is why his last letter astonished me. I had postponed telling Paul that I would not return to Tangier, but he ferreted out my decision from friends. He wrote me a tender letter saying: 'Now when I go in to your apartment, your personality is so strong, I cannot believe you will not return.' The Paul Bowles I know is not the cold fish that he has often been labelled but a warm and feeling friend whom I miss seeing.

Gavin Lambert

It seems appropriate that we first met at the house of Christopher Isherwood and Don Bachardy in Santa Monica, California; for Christopher and Paul had first met in Berlin in 1931, and Christopher chose Sally Bowles's second name for two reasons – he liked the sound of it and the looks of its owner. Almost forty years later (autumn 1968), Paul had returned to the United States for a few months, as visiting professor at San Fernando Valley State College, lecturing on the modern European novel, and – as he added with a twinkle of horror, 'something they call advanced narrative writing'.

The alert composure, and the wary ironic interest with which his eyes viewed the world, seemed very like his prose. He also had the aura of a profoundly displaced person – and not just because he was in a country where he had long ceased to feel at home. One other remark, but not its context, I remember from that evening: 'The outsider always *sees* more than the man in the crowd.'

Some years later, when I was living in Tangier and saw a good deal of Paul, I read *The Sheltering Sky* again and was struck by the epigraph from Kafka that heads the last section: *From a certain point onward there is no longer turning back. That is the point that must be reached*. And for Paul, I realized, the point was way off the map, on the far side of pessimism, somewhere beyond despair and hope. Not easy to reach, and fairly bleak, but with a long and sometimes unexpectedly amusing view. Paul, like Kafka, has a marvellous sense of humour.

The apartment where he has lived for many years is on the top floor of a building that looks like any grim anonymous block you pass on the drive from any airport to any city. A pile of worn suitcases, mementoes of the once inveterate traveller, occupies most of the small hallway. In the living-room, ghostly daylight is filtered through a jungle of plants massed on the terrace outside. Time and neglect have made the whole building increasingly shabby, the elevator often breaks down, and once part of Paul's living-room ceiling fell in. But Paul himself has remained quietly neat and elegant, untouched by the surrounding decay, even welcoming it – as confirmation of one of his reasons for staying in Tangier and hardly ever leaving the place. Tangier, he believes, has changed less than most parts of the world, and is just slowly, irreversibly running down. Persisting identity, however frayed, is always better than change, which can only be for the worse.

Another reason he gives for staying in Tangier is that he will never be able to understand Moroccans, who keep him suspended between alarm and amused surprise. This is particularly true of his closest Moroccan friend, Mohammed Mrabet, whose stories he has recorded and translated. 'Perhaps what intrigues me most about him', Paul said one day, 'is that he's always telling me about some extraordinary, fantastic adventure or experience he's just had – and I never know whether to believe him or not.'

There is a charming Alice in Wonderland logic in the idea that the less you understand (and by implication) trust someone close to you, the more interesting he becomes. But it can have a reverse side as chilling as Paul's stories 'A Distant Episode' and 'The Delicate Prey'. Concerning the eagerness of some Moroccans to sodomize male infidels, he once told me: 'The pleasure they get from it is not, as the infidels believe, sexual. It's the opportunity to inflict what they conceive of as the ultimate insult.'

Like all great travellers, Paul created his own country. Although he writes about it as North Africa, and sometimes as Central America, its real location is the Tropic of Magic. For Paul, 'magic' is 'a secret connection between the world of nature and the consciousness of man'. It can be discovered only viscerally, not through the mind, so he has spent much of his life dreaming and imagining it, with fear and wonder, in the hope of cracking a secret that would give him 'wisdom and ecstasy – perhaps even death'.

The quest of a highly civilized man for an anti-civilized 'truth' has always given his work a dark yet lucid tension. It has also made him, as a person, uniquely and precariously free, indifferent to security, to moral judgments, even to regret, an emotion he finds 'meaningless'. 'You have to accept. . . .' Last year he accepted an invitation to go to Paris for a TV interview in connection with the première of the movie of *The Sheltering Sky*. But he had no wish to reacquaint himself with a city he once loved. It had surely deterio-rated, and in any case he didn't care to be reminded of his youth. So he stayed less than forty-eight hours, long enough to discuss the interview, record it and then buy a new cashmere dressing-gown. I like to imagine him wearing it now, sitting in that twilit Moroccan living-room – or better still, lying in bed at night, listening to a familiar sound of Tangier after dark, the continual and unsettling rhythm of drums.

Nicholas Lezard

Living Alone on the Fringes of Literature

It is not as a pioneer that you seek out Paul Bowles in Tangier, however much that's how you would like it to be. He is used to unannounced visitors. In his latest memoir, *Two Years Beside the Strait*, he complains: 'Scarcely an afternoon passes without a visit from someone I never saw before and probably shall never see again. Giving all this time makes life seem a static thing, as though an infinite number of years lay ahead.'

That was in 1989. Since then, rumours that Bertolucci was to film his first novel, *The Sheltering Sky*, have turned into much-trumpeted fact. He has appeared on the extraordinarily popular French literary programme *Apostrophes*. The Spanish director Pedro Almodóvar wants to film Bowles's favourite story, 'The Time of Friendship'. There has even been a *South Bank Show* devoted to him.

Despite this, there is a suspicion here that he exists only on the fringes of literature: there is no entry for him, for example, in Martin Seymour-Smith's otherwise monumentally exhaustive *Macmillan Guide to Modern World Literature*. The chances, in Britain, of hearing any of his musical works are, unless you are unusually diligent or lucky, nil.

He is hardly unknown in Tangier, though. On the morning I was to see him I was sitting at a café with a Moroccan who told me, out of the blue, that I must go and see 'the very famous American writer, Paul Holmes. Very good writer'.

'Bowles,' I said.

'Yes, Bowles. If you want, I can arrange for you to see him.'

When I explained that I was in fact going to see Bowles and that I had already arranged it, he was no more surprised than if I had said I might be going to have a look round the Casbah that afternoon. The impression is that every white visitor to Tangier not wearing shorts is off to see the author. When I stepped out of the taxi by his apartment block, a scruffy young teenager pointed at me and asked: 'Pol Bol?' I nodded, and he showed me up the stairs (the lift was broken) to Bowles's door. He refused to accept any money for his help (any tourist in Morocco can expect to be charged just for the privilege of being left alone).

Bowles lives in what, by Moroccan standards, is luxury, but by European standards looks cruelly indistinguishable from genteel poverty. The effect is heightened by his appearance: answering the door himself, wrapped in a dressing-gown and bent rectangular with sciatica.

'I don't understand why the people who come to interview me complain about the apartment. They expect me to live in some kind of splendour. For some reason the French are the worst. They seem almost personally affronted. How can I clean this place up when I'm this ill?'

He sighs and gets back into bed. Despite the pleasant spring weather, the curtains are drawn and a fire has been lit. He speaks quietly but carefully, in tones modulated by almost superhuman patience and courtesy. It is difficult not to feel embarrassed and superfluous, having asked him to relinquish some of the tiny amount of free time he gets these days. Nor can it be much fun being ill in a Muslim country.

'The idea here is that if you're ill, it's the will of Allah and there's nothing much you can do about it. Try not to get sick or have an accident here. If you go to a hospital you'll have to arrange your own food and blankets. I've gone to a hospital and seen people who've been in road accidents just lying on the floor.'

This is a rather crucial point. His stories are almost all explosions of any cosy Western notions about the exotic attraction of travel through alien cultures. In calm, flat prose, his American heroes and heroines, all deluded about their motives for escape, are robbed, raped, tortured or killed so regularly that the first moral that can be drawn from his stories is: 'Stay at home'.

Yet Bowles has done no such thing. He is one of the last of the compulsive peripatetics. He is intensely aware of the dangers inherent in Western attitudes to other countries. (Gore Vidal described him as 'a man completely devoid of bullshit'; he is also a writer completely devoid of bullshit.) Bowles, I happen to know, does not reply to questions that begin with the word 'why', on the grounds that the answers can never be truthful. But why does he live in Tangier? Why live in a Muslim country? He is quietly proud of being apolitical and an atheist.

'I suppose it's the one thing I've got to thank my father for, not having to believe in God. . . .' And yet his closest Moroccan friend, Mohammed Mrabet, is a devout Muslim who, during Ramadan, has been known to denounce Bowles's visitors as Jews who ought to be killed for polluting the air breathed by Muslims. We can file this as aggravated bravado, but outbursts like that cannot make life easy.

'Well, I don't think I'd want to live anywhere else now. I don't want to go back to America, it's terrible over there now. I don't want to go to the Far East. And I certainly don't want to go to, uh, South Africa.' As an answer this is not quite as satisfactory as the epigraph to Book III of his novel *The Spider's House*, taken from the 'Song of the Swallow' in *The Thousand and One Nights*: 'To my way of thinking, there is nothing more delightful than to be a stranger. And so I mingle with human beings, because they are not of my kind, and precisely in order to be a stranger to them.'

Bowles is not given to grand pronouncements on the state of the world or literature. Who is he reading at the moment?

'Well, there's this book by an Englishman I was given. I don't know if you've heard of him – Peter Ackroyd. *Hawksmoor*, I think it's called. I must say that I don't understand what he's trying to say at *all*. For me it's meaningless.'

There is still the quality of benign evasion, familiar to anyone who has read his autobiography, *Without Stopping*, a thoroughly enjoyable book that has the air of having been written more to satisfy a contractual obligation than from any great urge to tell the world about himself; William Burroughs dubbed it *Without Telling*. He is a man not only devoid of bullshit, but also, it seems, of ego. His best stories are stories about not belonging, and he allows you to cultivate the suspicion that he does not belong anywhere himself. He exists in his writing, in his music. Even there you will not learn much about him. And why, you half expect him to ask, should you want to?

Marguerite McBey

My husband and I lived in Tangier for a long time before we met the Bowleses. In fact, it must have been after my husband's death in 1959, when I was seeing a lot of David Herbert, that I met them.

Both Jane and Paul came to lunch with me often and I painted them both several times. I drove them to town on one occasion and when I got to the Place de France, I asked them where they wanted to be dropped. This started a long discussion in the back of the car, which went on interminably, while I drove round and round and they discussed and discussed.

I am very fond of Paul, although during the many times I've seen him he has never said anything I've treasured or cared to repeat. But I do think he is fond of me and this sentiment is certainly returned. I love his books and could go on for ever painting his face.

I was at a small luncheon with Paul, two men and two other women. Someone remarked how Picasso had so changed the world with his paintings that it would never be quite the same again. Someone politely remarked: 'So has Mr Bowles.'

Paul was cutting a very tough piece of meat. He put down his knife and quietly said: 'But I never meant to.'

Joseph A. McPhillips III

I first met Paul Bowles in the summer of 1962. Since then our friendship has grown not only personally, but I suppose professionally, as Paul has done the music for five plays in which I directed the students of the American School of Tangier.

When I arrived in Tangier, I realized that Paul had composed the music for *The Glass Menagerie*, but I was unaware of how extensive his Broadway experience had been. He had written the music for three plays produced by Orson Welles, for plays by William Saroyan, and of course went on to compose music for Tennessee Williams's *Summer and Smoke*, *Sweet Bird of Youth*, and *The Milk Train Doesn't Stop Here Any More*. He also did music for documentary films and the film version of Lillian Hellman's *Watch on the Rhine*. (It was only after a lawsuit that he received credit for having done so.)

Besides his work in the theatre, of course, Paul has written chamber music, orchestral music and solo music for various instruments, particularly the piano. When I decided to direct the Yeats version of Sophocles' *Oedipus* in 1966, I asked him to write the music. He agreed, setting the choral odes to music. For my second production in 1967 he recorded background music for an adaptation he had done of his short story, 'The Garden'. For Euripides' *The Bacchae* (1969) he 'designed' music, if you will, using a dozen Moroccan musicians and training them in rhythmic patterns unfamiliar to their traditional music. He also used songs and taped incidental flute music. In *Orestes* (1978) he composed electronic music, taking sounds from diverse sources; dripping water or a tapping pencil. He would then elongate or shorten the sound at will.

Because I had an exceptionally gifted music teacher at the school who was able to train students to perform on drums and other

76

percussive instruments, Paul composed music for the guitar and drums for Camus's *Caligula* (1978).

In 1984, I adapted Jane Bowles's short story 'Camp Cataract', and it was produced along with her short play, *A Quarreling Pair*. *A Quarreling Pair* was conceived and performed in New York as a puppet play with two songs that Paul had written – 'My Sister's Hand in Mine' and 'The Frozen Horse'. Unfortunately, when I went into rehearsal, Paul had lost the second song. However, he composed another one. Both were played on the piano.

In the spring of 1992 he composed music for Euripides' *Hippolytos*, using a synthesizer. I believe he first encountered a synthesizer when Horowitz brought one to Tangier to work on the music for *The Sheltering Sky*.

Paul is an exceptionally gifted composer for the theatre. He senses the dramatic moment in a production that needs musical expression. I recall when Caligula begins to caress (and then strangle) Caesonia, the music sounds like the rattling of a snake when he first touches her, and is followed by a melancholy melody played on the guitar.

Besides his genius as a musician, Paul is great fun to work with and always accommodating. He is totally open to a director's suggestions and requests and seems immediately to understand what is needed. I saw him irritated only by the inability of singers to carry a tune or hit the right notes. He seems to enjoy the whole experience of putting on a play, appreciating the tension and wondering if it will all come together and work. He likes games, and perhaps a theatrical production is a game of chance in its final success or failure.

I recognize in my experience of working with Paul his supreme professionalism and his generosity. His music was written for the American School of Tangier, and of course no fees or financial benefits have ever been mentioned. These pieces have been done for the school as a donation. I can imagine few professional musicians or composers who would freely give of their time and creativity without financial consideration.

Paul is a gentleman, with superb manners and courtesy towards others. I think his deserved recognition of the past few years has fatigued him only because of the unceasing American and European media curiosity. He is incapable of saying no to interviewers or visitors or simply the curious.

I agree with Ezra Pound that an artist's work should speak for itself and that anecdotes and observations of the artist personally are really beside the point. I have known and seen Paul regularly for almost thirty years now, and it seems fatuous for me to recount episodes that testify to a friendship which covers a wide range of reactions to one another and experiences. He is a man of immense talent, of clear intelligence, and he has been a loyal friend.

Peter Owen

Who Is Paul Bowles?

1

In 1962 I was holidaying in a Moroccan mountain resort, Xauen,
not far from Tangier. My wife Wendy and I were talking to an
American about *The Sheltering Sky*, which we all greatly admired
and thought epitomized Morocco. Our new friend told us that Paul
Bowles lived in Tangier, and that as we were going there shortly,
we ought to try to meet him. He even suggested the American
Consulate would have his telephone number. So we telephoned the
Consulate, who were obliging, and even told us that his apartment
was quite close to them.

We did not then know that Paul and Jane had separate apartments in the same thirties' type apartment block. Paul refused to
have a telephone, and still doesn't have one, but Jane did. We rang,
explaining we were not only fans but that I was a publisher, and a
voice (later we realized it as Jane) said that if we'd ring back, she
would ask Paul if and when we might call. An appointment was
made for late afternoon.

When we got there, we found a middle-aged woman with a limp,
who introduced herself as Mrs Bowles, and a plain Moroccan
woman dressed in a kaftan. We later discovered this was Sherifa,
Jane's maid and occasional lover. There was a certain amount of
whispering between the two women before Paul arrived. My first
impression of Jane was that she was not particularly friendly, but I
did not know that she had recently been very ill, and also that she
tried to protect Paul from intruders whenever possible.

After an interval Paul appeared: he was slim, fair-haired and
spoke with a slight American accent. He has changed little in
the intervening years, and has always been neatly and elegantly
dressed. He has a stock of silk shirts which were made for him in

Thailand and other Eastern countries. Paul was, as he always is, polite and friendly. He seemed pleased that we liked *The Sheltering Sky*, which was much less well known than it is now. I told him about my publishing house, and said that if he ever had a book we could publish, I should be delighted to consider it. After a bit more talk, he remembered that he had collected some of his travel articles, which he thought might make a book. Would I like to take the manuscript away? That was *Their Heads Are Green*, which I published in 1963.

Paul has always been diffident and he often waits for his publishers to appear in Tangier before he volunteers to show them his manuscripts. It was as a result of visits to him during the past four years that I secured the stories for two collections, *Call at Corazon* and *A Thousand Days for Mokhtar*, as well as his journal, *Two Years Beside the Strait*. I suppose that, having lived for so long in Tangier, he does not have Western competitiveness and sense of urgency. He has always been suspicious of the mail, as he maintains that letters and packets are often lost. Other residents of Tangier share this distrust of his. Paul seems to believe that if he posts a manuscript or one of his rare first editions, that is the last he will ever see of it. He is often without file copies of his own books.

About two years later Wendy and I returned to Morocco and spent a few days in Tangier. The hotel we had previously used was full and Paul very helpfully suggested and reserved rooms in another. We met him and Jane and during the course of our visit Paul asked why I did not publish Jane's book. I said 'What book?', not having heard of *Two Serious Ladies*, which had appeared in the United States in 1943, when Jane was in her twenties, and which had become a cult book. Copies were virtually unobtainable. All this was explained to me by Paul, as they had no file copy. Jane had given her last copy to Ruth Fainlight Sillitoe, whom she had befriended when the Sillitoes lived in Tangier. It was suggested that Ruth might be persuaded to let me look at this rare volume.

On my return to London I contacted Ruth and Alan. Ruth was indeed reluctant to lend me her signed copy of Jane's book. (Jane inscribed very few books, especially since her illness, which made writing difficult.) Ruth was worried that I might not return the volume. I persuaded her that I was not a book thief. She knew it would be good for Jane if the book was revived.

Wendy and I read *Two Serious Ladies* and realized immediately that it was extra special, and so I contracted to publish it. I pointed out to Paul that it would be useful to get some pre-publication praise from eminent people. The book appeared in 1965, with quotes on the dust-jacket from Tennessee Williams, James Purdy, Alan Sillitoe and Francis Wyndham. It received an exceptionally good press.

We returned to Morocco in 1966. By this time I had got to know Paul and Jane and liked them both. Jane must always have had problems, but these were now exacerbated by her bad health and fragile mental state. She lacked self-confidence, had obsessional symptoms, and since her stroke suffered from occasional epilepsy, which frightened her. She was a warm and caring woman. Perhaps she had been too pampered by her doting widowed mother and by Paul, which made her less able to cope with day-to-day problems. She was pleased with the reception her book received in England and I believe it helped her self-esteem.

At this time Paul had rented a villa on 'the Mountain', where he was working on a book. We went there, and Jane and the maids brought along a picnic lunch, as Paul did not cook at the villa. I believe it was during that visit that I asked if I could handle world translation rights in Jane's book. Paul recommended Jane to agree. I have subsequently sold *Two Serious Ladies* and Jane's later book of stories, *Plain Pleasures*, to countries throughout the world.

I asked Jane if she was writing anything else, and some stories were mentioned. Paul volunteered to help her put together a selection for another volume and to advise her on the completion of one of the stories. My firm published *Plain Pleasures* in 1966. I wonder if, without Paul's efforts, Jane would ever have bothered to search out the stories, which she had put away.

I also published the first book by Paul's Moroccan friend, Mohammed Mrabet, which Paul had translated from tapes and put together. Jane appeared not to like Mrabet, and told me that Paul should be concentrating on his own writing rather than transcribing Mrabet's. She also pointed out that the books were stylistically Paul's. I recall that there was a certain amount of tension on the way to the Mountain, as Mrabet and Sherifa did not get on, and Jane was worried there might be trouble ahead. However, we spent a peaceful afternoon in the villa garden.

Wendy had then written her first novel, *There Goes Davey Cohen*, and Paul agreed to read it and give her a quote for the dust-jacket, if he liked it. He did.

Jane and Paul were invited to the annual party of a Swiss baroness; it was the party of the year. Jane invited us, having asked permission, and her instructions to us were that we should wear our oldest clothes. I assumed it was a hippie gathering and took her at her word. Jane was appalled by my very scruffy shirt, and said she hadn't meant to be taken quite so literally. After some thought she lent me a silk cravat of Paul's. Her own garb was a skirt and plain blouse, in contrast to the finery and lavish kaftans of most of the other guests. Paul and Jane left early but we enjoyed ourselves until late.

Tennesee Williams, a very old friend of the Bowleses, arrived with a female companion. Jane invited us all to dinner. The maids were given a night off, and Jane cooked a very good meal. (She had earlier professed that she was pretty useless as a cook.) Wendy remarked that it was the first meal she had fancied in Tangier. Jane had previously told me that Williams was travelling 'with a nice little drunk'. The lady turned out to be a formidable American matron. Jane was an excellent hostess, and we were served sitting on cushions. Tennessee drank a lot of vodka but said little. I hardly spoke to him until the end of the evening. He was charming. I thanked him for the quote he had given us for Jane's book. He told me it was his favourite book and deserved to become a classic.

We arranged to take Jane out to dinner on her own. We met at Guitta's, a restaurant much used by Europeans and close to Jane's apartment. But Guitta's was closed for dinner that evening and Jane couldn't make up her mind where else we should eat, which was one of the symptoms of her illness. In the taxi she said: 'Paul will be angry with me if I can't decide.' So she suggested the Parade Bar, where she was well known. Over a few glasses of wine I began to get to know her. She told me that she had always loved Paul and that he was the only man she had ever loved. She said that she had been propositioned by other men, including writers she admired, but would never have an affair with another man, as Paul would be too upset.

Jane had many friends in Tangier who were devoted to her. One of her oldest friends was David Herbert; David and Paul were both regular visitors when she was a patient at the hospital in Malaga.

I saw Jane again on another visit. It was probably two years later. She had just returned from Malaga, having had shock treatment. She was frail, but mentally in the best state in which I had ever seen her. She and Paul were being interviewed by a contingent of people from *Time* magazine. The reporter was accompanied by a photographer from the London office and his girl-friend. Jane's work had just been 'rediscovered' in the United States. Roger Straus had bought her novel, stories and play, *In the Summer House*, over lunch, without reading them, and told me he would publish them all in one volume. The book appeared under the title *The Collected Works of Jane Bowles*, to which Truman Capote contributed an introduction. The *Time* reporter had not bothered to read any of Jane's work, nor I believe Paul's, hoping to get 'cribs' in Tangier. Both Paul and Jane were very patient and did not seem to be surprised by this.

During our visit Jane organized parties for us, hosted by her friends, including David Herbert, as Jane was not well enough to entertain at home. Although all this must have been a strain, Jane coped with it well. She dressed up in a gorgeous kaftan for one dinner party. She could still look attractive when she bothered, and at that time usually wore a wig. Many women wore wigs in the sixties, but I am sure Jane would have thought visits to Moroccan hairdressers an ordeal.

It was at a dinner party, the last time I was to see Jane, that I said to her: 'Would you rather have been as you are or a cabbage?' Without hesitation she answered 'a cabbage'. Jane drank alcohol but disapproved of drugs, even hashish. The doctors had told her that she could have only one glass of wine. This distressed her, and she watered it to make it last longer.

Soon afterwards Jane started to deteriorate. I think she was pleased with her belated success and the various foreign translations, but it came too late, since by then she was very ill. I always felt that if she had found herself in a bourgeois milieu she might perhaps have become a housewife. Her family were bourgeois American Jews, and she had ambivalent feelings towards her mother, who was obviously very possessive.

I once asked Paul if Jane would have written but for him. His answer was that Jane wrote first, and that he followed.

I saw Paul at least once in Morocco during Jane's hospitalization in Malaga. He was lonely and missed her, but carried on his life much as before. He had a parrot of which he was fond, and on one visit it had disappeared. It died, and Paul thought that Sherifa had poisoned it. Before she went to Malaga, Jane dismissed Sherifa, who she feared was trying to poison her, as did Paul.

After Jane died Wendy and I came back to Morocco. Paul looked very ill and thin and told me that Jane's death was the worst thing that had ever happened to him.

I travelled to Tangier in the seventies to read the first part of Paul's autobiography, *Without Stopping*. He had written the first part about his childhood and family. When I told him how good I considered it and how vividly he had re-created his relatives, he smiled and said: 'Yes, weren't they awful?' In this part of the book he is candid, but in the later sections the characters do not come alive, as he doesn't flesh them out. Paul is too nice to write a real autobiography, as he is rarely nasty about anyone. He did not want to write the book but was persuaded to do so by an American publisher, and he accepted an advance which he tried to repay. But the publishers said he could do it the way he wanted. Paul told me that if they thought he would reveal everything about Jane, they were mistaken.

One of the few people Paul was sharp about was Anaïs Nin, whom he and Jane knew. Anaïs told me that she had written to Jane about her book 'as one writer to another'. I asked Paul about this, but he claimed the letter was so critical that it had made Jane ill.

Paul still lives in the same apartment. He lives simply. He sometimes has a daily maid, and his one luxury is a car, and the chauffeur he has employed for many years. Mrabet also visits him regularly. He leads an ordered life, going to bed late and rising late. He does not cook and relies on others to do this for him. He drives to the market and post office daily to buy necessities and to collect his mail. As he has no telephone he is at the mercy of callers, to whom he is unfailingly civil. He rarely goes to restaurants, and he will go only to those run by Europeans. He, as was Jane, is suspicious of local bars and restaurants. One exception is a Moroccan tea garden idyllically situated facing the sea, where he sometimes takes visitors to drink mint tea and to admire the view.

In 1988 I called on Paul. His friend, the composer Phillip Ramey, who rented Jane's old apartment every summer, told me that Paul had written a journal, which Paul diffidently gave me. I took it back to the hotel to read. I thought it was too short, but Jan, my present wife, enthused over it and suggested that I try to persuade him to add to it, as it should be published, whatever its length.

Paul finished off the entries for the journal that year. My firm published it as *Two Years beside the Strait* in 1990, in hardback, paperback and in a limited signed edition, which was oversubscribed. It has since been published in the United States, France and elsewhere. He wrote to me in 1989 to say that he was thinking of writing another autobiography 'to set the record straight'.

When Paul Bowles was asked a question by Melvyn Bragg, who interviewed him for the *South Bank Show*, he replied: 'It's all in the books.'

But is it?

2

In December 1991 I visited Tangier specifically to interview Paul for this book. Contrary to his normal custom, he agreed to see me at 11 a.m., as I had asked him if we could talk without the presence of his usual entourage.

I had a list of prepared questions and answers. I was not, however, surprised when Paul evaded some but answered others freely.

I arrived at the same time as a young Moroccan woman, whom I at first mistook for a student. The bell was not working – it had been disconnected – and she banged on the door intermittently for a few minutes. Eventually Paul opened the door (I was a little early); he was not yet fully dressed. The girl was his daily maid. He had already lit a log fire – the only heating in the living-room – as it was a cold day. He apologized for not being ready. There had been no recent recurrence of the crippling sciatica; he seemed spry, and sat on a low cushion on the floor – there are only cushions and a settee. He has regular massage which he believes controls the sciatica.

I first asked Paul if he regards himself as a survivor of the old world or a bridge into the future. He said that he sees himself as a survivor of the old, despite his material – drugs, violence, bisexuality, much less in evidence when he wrote the books. Experimental writing is now stylistic. He pointed out that the French writers of the sixties were concerned only with style – they were sterile. I asked about the Beats who came to Tangier in the fifties, mainly to see Burroughs, who lived there. He said that Kerouac was stupid and had no grasp of language. Allen Ginsberg was more intelligent. Burroughs had a real sustained talent. Genet, whom he never met, was there several times. He was a real writer – a great stylist. His material was his life.

Does he think that a writer's life is his own business?

'Anything one might want to ask about the writer is in the work. All they have to do is read it to know how I live, my preferences, what my life has been. But in the work it has been transformed. If you analyse it you will find out about the person. The commercial biographers have not read the books. Their interest is in gossip and prurience. Millicent Dillon [who wrote a biography of Jane Bowles] just sat back and said: "Tell me about her." 'That makes it much easier. She had a terrible task and that deserved a certain amount of truth-telling.'

'Most writers lead the dullest lives. They spend most of their time sitting writing.'

Does kif have any effect on creativity? None. But it enables a writer to concentrate for longer periods. Did he take kif as soon as he tried it?

'No, it took years. It was in 1947 when I returned to Morocco, I grew to like kif. Finally, in Curaçao, I started to inhale. Kif is better than "hash". It is not as strong and has no side-effects.'

Had he always wanted to write? He wrote poetry since adolescence, and his first poem was published in a literary magazine when he was seventeen. He edited his college magazine but he had not thought of writing fiction. His first career was music, as a composer. In Europe he studied under Aaron Copland, who became a friend. He also enrolled for Nadia Boulanger's classes in Paris. Writing music was much harder work than writing books. But composing for the theatre was remunerative.

His New England family background was middle class. His father was a dentist who wanted to be a concert violinist but was prevented by his family. His mother had taught. He absconded to Europe without telling his parents. A friend who didn't like his family helped to get him a passport. Somehow he got the fare money together; he did not borrow it. Never! In Paris he got a job as a telephone operator at the *New York Herald Tribune*. He had learned French at school, so he was already proficient at the language, but it was not easy taking the calls.

Paul got to know Gertrude Stein in Paris, having written to her to request a contribution for his college magazine. She liked him and introduced him to her friends. She was very nice, although he believed she could be sharp with some people. Alice Toklas spoke little until Gertrude Stein died; she demurred to her friend. After Gertrude's death she never stopped talking.

Paul commuted between the United States and Europe. His father sent him money to come home. In 1931 he was in Berlin for a short period, where he got to know Spender and Isherwood. But it was a decadent scene. The country was obviously on the verge of collapse. Hitler was already being talked about but was not taken seriously. Paul soon returned to Paris, not liking Berlin.

He first visited Morocco in 1931 at the suggestion of Gertrude Stein. She said the sun shone all the time. Paul liked the colourful life, the costumes, dancing and the music. 'It was like a constant theatre.' He returned several times in the thirties and got to know Morocco and other parts of North Africa.

Paul regards writing itself as easy. It is finding relevant material that is hard. *The Sheltering Sky*, *Let It Come Down* and *The Spider's House* all flowed easily. *Up Above the World* was hard work.

He had visited the Sahara. He started *The Sheltering Sky* in New York. (I imagined what such a voyage would have been like with Jane. In fact she had never set foot in Africa, at that time.) The mother and son in the book were based on real people he had met. But the central characters were composite portraits of Paul and Jane.

He spent more than four years in Mexico in the thirties and early forties. Twenty years later he wrote *Up Above the World*, set in a Central American country. He was able to recapture the atmosphere which had so impressed him.

I asked him about 'Pages from Cold Point', a story about the seduction of a father by his son, which Norman Mailer hailed as one of the best stories ever written. That tale is a complete fantasy. Paul had spent two months in Jamaica – the background was real, but not the characters or the situation.

Is he happy about his image as a bisexual writer? He said he does not know much about it, but he thinks bisexuality is on the way out. Moroccan men and boys all used to sleep together, but they do so much less now. Paul had asked some of them, and they said it was no longer the 'mode'. Is this because of Aids? No, it had finished earlier.

He was not shocked by the *louche* life-style of the Stein ménage and their associates. He considered that people should be able to express themselves as they wished. That was a good thing.

After his marriage to Jane he had a short affair with Peggy Guggenheim in New York. She was impossible. Had he had many affairs? 'With women? Not many.'

He met Jane Auer in the thirties. They went to a party in Harlem where everyone smoked marijuana, even Jane, who had not smoked before. Jane said that Paul was her 'enemy'. Why? He thought she meant he had paid her too little attention. Soon they decided to travel to Mexico with friends. When Jane telephoned her mother to tell her, Mrs Auer suggested that she had better meet Paul.

In Mexico Jane disappeared, returning to the United States to stay with a friend. Later, she met Paul often and they decided to marry. As Jane's family were Jewish, I wondered how her mother had reacted. She asked Jane if she couldn't find herself a nice Jewish boy. There was someone hanging around who wanted to take her out. But Jane replied that she did not like Jews – 'She was quite anti-Semitic. She did not get on with her mother. They always had an ambivalent relationship.'

Jane had spent two years in a Swiss sanatorium for treatment of her tubercular leg. This left her with phobias – fire, dogs, sharks. Was it not frightening for two such complicated people to consider marriage? No, neither of them had any doubts – they liked each other. They were married the day before Jane's twenty-first birthday.

Jane had already written a novel in French while she was in the sanatorium, but she destroyed it. 'She wanted to destroy everything she wrote.' Soon she started writing her novel, *Two Serious Ladies*. It took three years; she wrote slowly. They went through it together. Paul was then writing music criticism. His main contribution to Jane's novel, he says, was to get her to cut a section which later became a short story, published in *Plain Pleasures*. The novel was originally going to be called *Three Serious Ladies*.

After Pearl Harbor, Paul returned to the United States from Mexico. He was interviewed for his suitability for military service but was rejected on psychiatric grounds. He saw the psychiatrist's notes, which stated 'Psychopathic personality'. Paul had told his interviewer that he could not sleep in a dormitory full of men. He had to sleep alone. He regarded other people as potential enemies. That dated from his childhood, when he locked his door against his parents, fearing they would kill him.

At the beginning of their marriage Jane and Paul shared a bedroom, but later they had separate rooms and he locked his door. He still does.

The theme of guilt recurs in his work. He says we all suffer from guilt as children, and that is carried through life. He did not much care for his father but liked his mother. Legacies from an aunt and his grandmother helped him. He could not have lived in the United States, although New England was better than New York. His only surviving relative is a second cousin. His parents did not want him to become an artist and were not impressed by his success.

He has never drunk much alcohol – he has the occasional glass of wine or Dubonnet – not even at parties. He regards the drinking in the Tangier social scene as 'crazy'. Jane's fear of kif was due to an overdose of *majoun*, which made her ill. Paul has never used hard drugs.

For a time, Jane and Paul shared the apartment in Immeuble Itesa. The small apartment on the top floor, which he now occupies, became vacant in the fifties, and he took it. At that time Jane had hired six maids who were sleeping on the floor in the main flat. It was pandemonium. Jane found them things to do, like delivering messages. They stole most of her things and some of his. Sherifa regarded herself as the maids' boss. 'She clapped her hands for them to bring her breakfast in bed.' Paul had to get away.

I told him that Jane said to me she did not like Mrabet (his long-time Moroccan friend). Paul was surprised – when Jane was very ill, Mrabet was the only one who could get her to do things. She threw food at the wall that Paul brought her, and Mrabet talked to her quietly. She did not want to behave badly in front of him, as 'he wouldn't understand'. It was Jane who first met Mrabet, when he was a barman at a friend's house. Paul hoped that Mrabet would become his chauffeur. He took him to the United States to drive him around. It was cheaper than hiring an American driver, since it cost only Mrabet's fare and keep, no salary.

After Jane died, Paul wrote very little. He had no incentive. She had been a catalyst. Recently he completed a short novella. He is translating a new novel by a talented young Guatemalan writer, Rodrigo Rey Rosa, from Spanish. He has also been working over some of his music. Many people come to interview him. It takes up a lot of his time, and he finds it difficult even to find time to write letters. While I was there two Frenchmen arrived without warning and requested an interview later that week. He had another appointment with a journalist that day.

At about 1 p.m. he retired to bed so that the maid could bring his lunch – the usual routine. We continued to talk in his bedroom. He did not mind answering questions while he ate. He is used to it. I asked him if he wanted to move into a centrally heated house with servants. No, he prefers staying where he is. Perhaps he would not mind if someone moved all his books and belongings, but he believes he could not afford the upkeep of a house. He would not want to change his life, in hindsight. He mentioned an acquaintance who had committed suicide. We agreed that everyone has the right to do what they want with their own life.

When Paul Bowles came to Tangier in 1931 he rented a cheap house on the Old Mountain. (This is now the most fashionable area, where only the very rich live.) Aaron Copland also lived there. They managed to acquire a piano. There were a lot of French people in Tangier and it was easy to buy Western accoutrements. In the intervening years the town has grown out of recognition, and not for the better.

Morocco is still riddled with superstition. Jane's maid, Sherifa, placed a nasty 'magic' mess (congealed blood, hair, etc.) under a potted plant, hoping it would influence Jane to give her money. When Jane was in the Malaga hospital, Paul, not knowing about the 'spell', tried to remove the plant to his apartment. Sherifa went berserk and attempted to gouge out his eyes with her fingers. He fled, but later retrieved the plant, which he still has.

I asked him for his views on homosexuality and bisexuality. Moroccan men are traditionally bisexual. The only things Paul disapproves of are paedophilia and 'liberation movements'. He did not elaborate further.

Did he like the film of *The Sheltering Sky*? It is too long and digresses from the book. I pointed out that Malkovitch was unlike Bowles in his portrayal. 'He didn't like the book or the part.' He is not writing anything now. 'It is always hard finding the right material.' Writing itself and evoking places are not difficult – 'the atmosphere of Mexico was firmly embedded in my mind'; years later he used this atmosphere, too.

I pointed out he is considered enigmatic and difficult to interview or get to know. He was genuinely surprised. 'It's just not true. I don't know why people say that.' Yet among his acquaintances in Tangier he is considered to be reticent and reclusive.

We discussed the future of books. Paul believes that in fifty years' time books will no longer be read. 'It will be video cassettes. People won't want to read. They will see images instead. Education in every country is growing worse each year. Fewer and fewer people have any understanding of language. The visual side will take over. Television is taking over everything. The recent French "experimental" writers were rearguards fighting against what went before.'

I asked if there was anything else he wanted to say.

'Yes. What has happened in my career is all explained by one word – luck. Good luck. It was always a matter of luck with me.'

I suggested that perhaps skill and intelligence had something to do with it. But he insisted – 'luck'.

Would I find a taxi nearby? Smiling, he replied: 'That's like asking me if I'll go to Heaven!'

James Purdy

Carl Van Vechten invited me to meet Paul Bowles one evening. I was at the beginning of my own career as a writer, and was a bit nervous at meeting so mysterious and legendary a figure as Mr Bowles. My apprehension was put at an end when I met him. He seemed like a quiet, very dignified and kind man, perhaps like a doctor of medicine. It was also heartening to learn that he admired my first book, *63: Dream Palace*, which had recently appeared for the first time in England.

Since our meeting in Carl Van Vechten's house, we have been in steady correspondence. One of the most interesting things about Paul Bowles is his reserve and distance. Since my meeting with him so long ago nothing has changed that reserve and distance. His letters and our infrequent meetings are always like the first time, framed in the same cordial but distant and formal character as that of our first meeting in New York City.

Phillip Ramey

A Time of Friendship

Early in 1969, at a modern-music concert in New York, Aaron Copland introduced me to a handsome, elegantly dressed gentleman with grey hair. 'This', he announced, looking as satisfied as an owl that has caught an especially succulent mouse, 'is Paul Bowles.'

A few months before, Aaron had recommended Bowles's short stories and novels and lent me a couple of volumes. I read them with growing fascination, for they seemed unlike anything else. It was not long before I was familiar with almost everything Bowles had written.

Bowles at one time had studied music composition with Copland. The two were old friends. I knew that Bowles lived in far-off Tangier. Aaron used to say, in wonderment: 'Paul and I went to Morocco in 1931, and he's still there.' Thus I was startled suddenly to find myself face to face with my new favourite author. With the enthusiasm of youth, I declared: 'I'm happy to meet you, Mr Bowles, because I've read your books and think they're original and wonderful.' The great man smiled coolly, took a languid puff from his cigarette-holder, and replied: 'Ah, yes?' Not having seen each other in some time, he and Aaron began a lengthy conversation. Twice I dared to interject a comment; twice Bowles looked my way but said nothing. Later, in a snit at being excluded, I complained to Aaron: 'Well, Paul Bowles certainly did not find *me* of any interest.' Aaron, amused, said soothingly: 'Don't be upset. Paul's always been something of a cold fish.'

When, thirteen years later in 1982, I decided to vacation in Morocco, Copland suggested visiting Bowles in Tangier, and a colleague who was to accompany me expressed enthusiasm for the idea. I was reluctant, remembering my less-than-gratifying encounter with the expatriate writer and composer. I reasoned that if Bowles, who had the reputation of being a recluse, was fond of

93

visitors – in our case, unexpected visitors – he would hardly have isolated himself for decades in Morocco without a telephone. So when, after enjoying the sights of Marrakesh, Fez and Meknes, we arrived in Tangier, I had pretty much determined to forgo seeing him. Our room, high in the Rembrandt Hotel, had an impressive view of the harbour and the Strait of Gibraltar; there was another medina to explore, another casbah to investigate and more Arab coffee-houses in which to drink mint tea. It was *safi*, enough. Why ruin our stay by invading a stranger's privacy and being made to feel unwelcome? 'Look, I don't think this is a good idea – it's too pushy,' I said. 'Let's leave Mr Paul Bowles to his splendid isolation.' My colleague, a diminutive, rather humourless fellow who tended to be pleased with himself and found it difficult to imagine he might not be welcome everywhere, wasn't having that. 'We're going,' he snapped. 'I have the address, and we're going.'

Fortunately (or, I thought at the time, unfortunately), the taxi-driver knew the location of Immeuble Itesa, as Bowles's Führer-bunkeresque apartment building is called. The door to his flat was opened by a compact Moroccan with a villainously friendly smile, who introduced himself as Mohammed Mrabet and retreated into the kitchen to brew tea. I recognized the name – Mrabet is one of several native story-tellers whose works Bowles has translated into English – and I said to myself, ye gods, what a place: even the famous author's houseboy writes books!

In his dark, cavelike *sala*, the man whom the *Boston Globe* designated 'a literary god' sat on a floor cushion, contentedly smoking from his holder. My colleague and I introduced ourselves, and Bowles politely directed us to other cushions. Mrabet appeared with cups of tea and then began to puff at his *sebsi*. After some desultory conversation, silence fell. It occurred to me that I had travelled several thousand miles and tracked Bowles to his lair only to receive a further dose of indifference. As I began to plan revenge on my colleague, I heard him proclaim to Bowles that we were musicians, and that we brought greetings not only from Copland but from another friend, the composer-critic Virgil Thomson. At once Bowles's interest was engaged, and the ice melted. He had assumed, I think, that we were the usual book fans, come to offer platitudes about his best-known novel, *The Sheltering Sky*; we would have our tea and depart, and he would breathe a sigh of relief. Music, however, was another matter.

During the next few days we visited Bowles regularly and discovered that he was always ready to discuss music and musicians.
With his permission, we rummaged through his manuscripts, and
he gave to my colleague, who was at that time a pianist, an unpublished piece; and to me a record of himself reading some of his
stories, along with a note for Copland.

I didn't expect to see Morocco or Bowles again. But he and I
exchanged a few letters, and when planning a trip to Lisbon two
years later I couldn't resist a cheap air-fare to Tangier. So, I found
myself once more at his door, this time not at all apprehensive and
free of that tiresome if useful colleague. Bowles didn't seem displeased to see me. I had brought tapes of musical works with which
he was unfamiliar, having been cut off to great degree from Western
concert music since removing himself to Morocco in 1947. I was
amazed that he did not know, for instance, Copland's classic *Appa-
lachian Spring* – which he termed 'one of the most beautiful pieces
I've ever heard, but twice too long' (Copland's laughing retort
when I told him: 'Too late now!'). Nor was he really familiar with
the *Short Symphony* – 'Aaron was working on that here, in Tangier,
on our out-of-tune piano up on the Mountain, but I never heard an
orchestra play it.' Or several late pieces by Stravinsky, who is
perhaps his favourite composer.

During the past several years, drawn by an agreeable climate, the
possibility of peace and quiet for work and an evolving friendship
with Bowles ('Make many more trips to T.,' he commanded in a
1985 inscription in his *Collected Stories 1939–1976*), I have spent
every summer in Tangier, often in the apartment directly beneath
him, where his late wife, the writer Jane Bowles, used to live. It is,
naturally, a pleasure to see him every day for months at a time; we
have even concocted a system of rhythmic taps on the walls to
signal when either of us wants to visit.

My days are spent at the little concert hall of the French Cultural
Centre, an ideal place for composing. In late afternoon I sometimes
go with Paul to the colourful Fez Market, in his golden, vintage
1966 Mustang, with the redoubtable Abdelouahaid Boulaich, his
long-time driver, at the wheel. For company in the evenings, aside
from Paul, I can usually rely on getting together with friends who
live in or regularly visit Tangier, at restaurants (especially the one
run by the hospitable Mercedes Guitta), cafés, beach bars and
private homes. Among these people are David Herbert, second son

of the fifteenth Earl of Pembroke, whom Paul has described as the city's 'unofficial social arbiter'; the young Guatemalan writer Rodrigo Rey Rosa, whose books Paul has translated; the American painter and writer Buffie Johnson, who has often allowed me the use of her apartment; the English writer and adventurist Gavin Young; the Italian composer and Trieste Opera director, Baron Raffaello de Banfield; Paul's preferred French translator, Claude-Nathalie Thomas; the British-born novelist, biographer and screenwriter Gavin Lambert; the American poet Ira Cohen; the English tycoon Martin Soames; the former director of Tangier's French Cultural Centre, Georges Bousquet; an American college student, Kenneth Lisenbee, whom Bowles in one of his books nicknamed 'Krazy Kat' after the 1920s cartoon character; the American photographer Cherie Nutting; the Moroccan musician from Jajouka, Bachir Attar, who has recorded with the Rolling Stones; and the young American playwright Steven Diamond, inclined to make flying visits from Indonesia. Many of these friends were introduced to me over the years by Paul, for it seems that anyone of interest who arrives in Tangier eventually gravitates to his apartment.

Paul and I occasionally exchange books and discuss authors (we share, for example, a taste for the psychological suspense novels of Patricia Highsmith and Ruth Rendell, and the literate thrillers of Graham Greene and Norman Lewis), and he enjoys gossip, especially if *louche* or grotesque. But the main topic is usually music: his, mine, that of our various contemporaries. This is perhaps what sets me apart from his other friends in Tangier. We often listen to music together. He has long had a machine to play cassette tapes and now there is one for compact discs.

If, as the American composer, essayist and one-time Tangier resident Ned Rorem has proposed, all concert music is either of French or German orientation, then Paul's personal taste runs – as does his music – decidedly to the former. Ravel, Poulenc and Copland please him, Beethoven, Mahler and Schoenberg do not. He likes music that charms, and has aimed for that effect in his own scores, which are often inflected by jazz and blues (for instance, the *Six Latin-American Pieces* for piano, the *Concerto for Two Pianos, Winds and Percussion*, many of the songs). In considerable contrast are his novels and stories, in which the atmosphere sometimes verges on the horrific. Once, I asked him about this strange dichotomy, and he explained: 'The music and the books come from different compartments of the brain. They are quite separate.' In creating fiction, he said, one inevitably writes about people, and 'hostility can emerge'. Conversely: 'Music is about music – a closed cosmos existing only in musical terms.'

When not listening to music, Paul is obsessively given to tapping out polyrhythms with his fingers, even drumming on the roof of his car during outings in the countryside. Although he has composed little during the last four decades, he retains a musician's most basic instincts. Still, he was annoyed by Rorem's odd prediction, in an article, that his light, entertaining music would outlast his serious, nihilistic fiction. 'Is that supposed to mean that my books are of no importance?' he asked.

In New York I meet many musicians, both composers and performers, and with pianists it seems natural to promote Paul's attractive keyboard music. Several years ago, I had a hand in arranging for some of it to be recorded on a Dutch label. More recently, Ramon Salvatore, an American pianist who has performed my own works, released an album that includes Paul's *Six Latin-American Pieces* and the first recording of *Carretera de Estepona*. In the summer of 1991, with the co-operation of the genial Georges Bousquet and the French Cultural Centre, Salvatore came to Tangier to present an all-American recital that featured several Bowles pieces (along with works by Copland, Virgil Thomson, John Corigliano and myself). Paul and I and Krazy Kat attended it together. The hall was packed with Moroccan, French and American residents (the English found other things to do) and a few dozen tourists, and the evening was a success despite an ancient, ailing piano. Paul was much applauded after his music was played, and again at the end of the concert. (For a poster announcing the singular, perhaps even historic, event, he had provided the following typically laconic statement, which was reproduced in his own handwriting: 'The composers represented on this unusual program, apart from being natives of the United States of America, have in common the fact that all of them, at one time or another, sojourned here in Tangier.')

Copland, as noted, thought Paul to be 'something of a cold fish'; and, certainly, an impression of dourness was widely disseminated a few years ago by the publication of an inaccurate and malicious biography. It is undeniable that many pictures show him looking grim, for he dislikes photo sessions. But there is another, very different side rarely seen by those who don't know him well – a

97

cordial, even affectionate, Paul Bowles, his manner spiked by a remarkable sense of humour. To illustrate: ever since Bernardo Bertolucci filmed *The Sheltering Sky* in 1990, Paul has been pestered not only by the usual visiting lunatics of every stripe, but by journalists, academics and documentary film-makers. Few of these strike him as being passably intelligent or congenial ('Journalists refuse to verify or check. They're certain they're right.'), but he is none the less always coolly polite. He does not relish being bored, however, and during late-night get-togethers at his flat with close friends, his acid-laced remarks about the day's intruders can be quite funny (as can his mimicking of the singular piping voices of such deceased celebrities as Truman Capote and Virgil Thomson).

In a special category are Paul's imitations of various unsavoury birds; his reproduction of the raucous 'speech' of various African Grey parrots that he has owned approaches high comedic art. There is also a story of which I never tire, in which Paul describes, with feline hisses and growls, how Henrietta, a Siamese cat belonging to the composer Peggy Glanville-Hicks, stalked him through room after room of her home, until in desperation he barricaded himself in a clothes-closet. Another tale concerns a Moroccan maid who was convinced that *djenoun* (evil spirits) lived in the cold-water pipes of Paul's apartment. One day he noticed her cleaning the toilet, cautiously removing water from the bowl with towels. When he pulled the chain to demonstrate a more sensible method, the rush of water so terrified the poor woman that she emitted a sonorous shriek (rendered spectacularly by Paul) and ran from the sinful Nazarene's flat, hysterically waving her arms in the air.

One evening Paul, Krazy Kat, Steve Diamond and I were walking to Casa Italia, a restaurant located in an old Moroccan palace not far from the Itesa. As we descended a steep, unlit street, we heard behind us a faint, somehow sinister, metallic sound, gradually coming closer. 'What's that?' asked Krazy Kat nervously. 'I don't know,' answered Steve. 'If we slow down until it catches up with us, we'll find out,' I suggested. Rolling out of the gloom came a solitary Coke can. It proceeded to keep pace with us. Whispered Paul: 'I think we're being bugged.'

He can also be amusing about himself. Cautious, to say the least, about his finances, he is fond of accusing me of 'spending money like a drunken sailor' – this, because I frequently dine out. One day, after he had grumbled about a one-dirham price rise (about twelve cents) for some household item at the Fez Market, Steve affectionately dubbed him 'The Cheapskate of Tangier'. Weeks later, Cherie happened to mention the city's most expensive and pretentious restaurant, which provoked me to put on a severe face and inquire of Paul: 'Just when, sir, are you going to treat all your friends to dinner at the Marquis?' His retort, delivered with the slyest of smiles, was: 'But how *could* I do such a thing? It would be too out of character for the Cheapskate of Tangier.'

Paul is literal-minded to a surprising degree, and therefore vulnerable to pranks. I didn't fully appreciate this until 1988, when a collection of his new short stories appeared. One story, 'Hugh Harper', concerns a British resident of Tangier whose eccentricity 'consisted in a taste for human blood', which he kept in the refrigerator and was in the habit of offering as refreshment to guests. This struck me as one of Paul's funniest tales. He said it had been inspired by an actual person. 'Should another vampire appear in Tangier,' I observed, 'it would serve you right if you were paid a visit.'

In the spirit of his story, I wrote him a preposterous letter on local hotel stationery, posting it as I left for a few days in Fez. It follows, grammatical, syntactical and orthographical grotesqueries intact:

Dear M. Bowles,

My nomen is Marjan C. van Vroonz of Utrecht. I am collectur of finger-nail, to-nail and the hair of noses of the great men. Also other things and liquids.

A delightsful woman – Mlle. Chérie Nooty – has telled to me that you emjoy provide her with to-nails and to write in your books of peoples drink blod for the apertif. May I to visit you soonest, extrat some to-nail and the other parts you permit, and to drink blod? Iam pay for do this, 50 Guilders, may be 100, if blod explode me.

I come you Samedi, at 5 afternoon with my machine. Plese to be not with clothes, and to be there disenfiction liquid, this important.

Good-By.

in respets,
Mlle. Marjan C. van Vroonz

Returning late that Saturday (Samedi) afternoon, I unpacked and went up to see Paul. For a long time there was no answer to my knocks. Then the door slowly opened, on the chain. Paul peered out apprehensively, and said: 'Oh, it's you. I was afraid it might be Mademoiselle van Vroonz.' Laughing, I responded: 'But surely you knew that letter was a joke, that *I'm* Mademoiselle van Vroonz!' In his best George Raft tough-guy voice, he shot back: 'Oh yeah? So where's your blood machine?'

During the fall and winter we keep in touch by mail (although, owing to the fantastical nature of the Moroccan postal service, letters can take anything from four days to four months arriving) and, sometimes, telephone. Paul's correspondence tends to be dry – or at least to the point. After he had endured three weeks of heavy winter rain:

> . . . I don't mind bad weather if I can stay in and be
> comfortable. But that was made impossible by copious leaks in
> the ceiling of every room, which resulted in lakes underfoot,
> rugs soaked, water running onto my bed. It rained day and
> night without cease. Mold grew in white fluffs on the
> furniture, the water dripped into the middle of the salon,
> undeterred by the fire in the fireplace. As I write this, there is
> no dry place to put my feet; the water drips regularly into a
> line of bowls and kitchen receptacles beside me. This house is
> clearly jinxed.

About my proposed plan – never, alas, implemented – to sabotage a recital by an ex-friend, a pianist whose trade mark is memory lapses, he wrote: 'I loved the idea of you seated in the front row at [his] concert, holding the scores in full view and evincing amazed disapproval throughout the duration of the music. It would make a very funny scene in a film.'

Learning I had attended a reading by a writer we both admire: 'So you finally met [X] – caught her in the undignified act of signing her books en masse. I wonder why she stoops to that, need of money?'

Responding – with what he termed 'my only limerick' – to a testy verse I sent him when the South African novelist Nadine Gordimer was awarded the 1991 Nobel Prize for Literature:

'There was a nice girl named Nadine
Who felt that mankind was unclean
A day is a night
And a black man is white
In Miss Gordimer's African scene.'

On the domestic front: 'I'm delighted with my new maid, now that the old one has made away with everything.' Also:

Abdelouahaid [Paul's driver] took it into his head to go out and buy me a new stove, claiming that the one I have now is no good. He's fairly right, but he just came to deliver a new one, which proved to be too big to fit into the place reserved for it, so he's gone away to look for another. Chaos in the kitchen! He was supposed to bring a chicken, but he failed to do that. A stove is so much bigger and more expensive. Unfortunately it's made of iron and enamel, and I can't have it for lunch.

Reacting to a piano piece (from my *Epigrams, Book 2*) dedicated to him: 'No. 5, *Demonic*, sounds the most difficult of the lot, but I imagine that's not what you want to know; rather whether I think it *ressemblant*. (Although it's not a portrait. It's the composer's idea of the subject, no?) In any case, it's pleasingly violent.'

Concerning an invitation to the West African nation of Mali, the scene of his recent short novel, *Too Far from Home*: 'That's all I need, to live in a place where the population is entirely animistic and the witch-doctors consult tortoises to help diagnose the ills of their patients. It might not be too different from Tangier.'

For Paul, in his favourite role of passive spectator, Morocco has been a congenial milieu – a continuous peep-show of the chaotic, where the delicious possibility of violence always lurks in the wings. The illogicalities of Muslim society, maddening to many Westerners, intrigue and amuse him. Writing in his autobiography, *Without Stopping*, of his initial visit so long ago to that extraordinary land, he approvingly notes its intrinsic theatricality, 'the impression of confusion and insanity'. 'I knew', he concludes, 'I would never tire of watching Moroccans play their parts.'

The essence of more than a few of his books has, after all, derived from nearly half a century's residence in Morocco. Even today, Paul will sometimes sit outside at the Café Tingis in Tangier's Zoco Chico, sipping a mint tea and noting the bizarre behaviour of denizens of the Medina. As he walks through the narrow Casbah alleys, his novelist's eye misses nothing: no drama goes unremarked, no peculiarity unseen, no lunacy unappreciated.

He complains that his adopted country – and especially Tangier, where ugly new high-rise buildings sprout everywhere and fast-food restaurants invade the once-classy Boulevard Pasteur – has become too modern and Americanized; that one must now travel far south, to the pre-Sahara, for remnants of the old, the primitive, the real. But despite this outrage (which may even gratify his innate pessimism – he calls it realism), I doubt he would be happier elsewhere. Never mind that his roof leaks, his maids steal, prices rise, doctors are homicidal and hordes of journalists beard him in his den; Paul Bowles lives on in Morocco.

Richard Rayner

Relishing the Abyss and the Furies

Paul Bowles is not just an outsider in American literature; he is an anachronism. Besotted with travel, he has lived outside the United States for most of his life and has continued to write in the ominous style that was at its most fashionable in the late forties and early fifties.

The American critic Theodore Solotaroff has dubbed this 'the algebra of nihilism'. Its practitioners were Mailer, Beckett, Sartre and Camus, among others, and Bowles, whose masterpiece, *The Sheltering Sky*, is a novel so black and shattering as to make *Nausea* and *The Naked and the Dead* seem by comparison the products of a boozy, almost benevolent, melancholy. One imagines the nihilists congregated in an ill-lit bar. "Yo, Sam, Bert, Paul, *boys*," says Mailer, slumped over a table of empty absinthe bottles, "I tell ya, that Bowles, *guys*, he really hit the jackpot." Beckett is silent.

Born in 1910 in Long Island, Bowles was published alongside Joyce, Breton and Stein in the Paris-based avant-garde magazine *transition* when still at high school and aged only 17. Thereafter he was to look to Europe and, ultimately, North Africa.

Given his upbringing, this is not surprising. He was the son of a dentist, a tyrant of drill and gas who (allegedly) put his six-week-old child outside the window on a freezing February night and who (definitely) forced him to chew each mouthful of food 40 times. This process was known, after its proponent Horace Fletcher, as Fletcherization, a useful description for the development of any oddball childhood.

Bowles was further Fletcherized by his mother, who sat at his bedside reading aloud the stories of Edgar Allan Poe. In his auto-biography, *Without Stopping*, Bowles describes how he did not so much listen to *The Fall of the House of Usher* and *The Tell-Tell Heart* as undergo them. *The Tell-Tale Heart* begins: "True –

nervous – very, very dreadfully nervous I had been and am; but why *will* you say that I am mad?" Strong meat for a young child and perhaps small wonder that Bowles's work would show such cold relish for the abysses and furies of the human mind.

Bowles did well at school, though his teachers may have been puzzled by the quote next to his photo in his high-school year book. It said: 'This strange disease of life.' The doomy and self-dramatizing existentialism arrived early and has stayed. He went to the University of Virginia where he studied English, French, geology and the history of music, and where he tossed a coin. He writes: 'Tails would have meant that I would have had to take a bottle of Allonal that night and leave no note. But heads meant that I would leave for Europe as soon as possible. . . .'

So he went to Paris, running off in secret. After that it was to and fro between New York and Europe and Morocco, meeting Gertrude Stein and Aaron Copland, who became a friend, and trying to decide whether he should be poet, composer or novelist. At this time he was more interested in the theory of art than art in action, in idleness than work, and mooned around like the hero of one of those André Gide novels he admired so much.

Copland warned Bowles that unless he went to work he would destroy himself by the time he was 30. Bowles made a choice. He would become a composer. Throughout the 1930s he wrote music on a bigger and bigger scale – for concerts, for plays, for films, for Orson Welles – pushing himself towards success. Then, in 1937, he met Jane Auer. She was 20, red-haired, petulant, brilliant, a would-be writer and an already accomplished drunk.

She had refused to go out with men, and yet the second time she met Bowles she agreed to go with him to Mexico. She was a lesbian; he was sexually uninterested, but with homosexual tendencies. The Mexican trip was a disaster – Jane ran off, was found sick in a seedy hotel – and they were married some six months later. She had told a friend: 'He is my enemy.'

Predictably enough, it was not a conventional marriage, although it *was*, in its weird fashion, a great love story. In *Without Stopping* Bowles describes how as a child he cultivated the skill of viewing, rather than participating in, his own existence. And in the marriage he lived to a large extent vicariously through Jane. She was the one who climbed over the edge of a roof to retrieve lost manuscript pages, who snatched a kitten away from a rattlesnake, who almost got herself killed in a brothel in Guatemala City.

Bowles watched it all, fascinated by the anarchic sense of adventure and the instability – she attempted suicide by slashing her wrists in 1942 – qualities which he would then try occasionally to control. She would then remind him of his pre-marital promise that each accept the other for what she was. For her, Bowles often represented the kind of authority which he had so hated in his own father; and yet she also hated it when he was displeased with her.

Often they would live apart, Jane having left with one of her lovers, and then she would come back. The relationship was nothing if not obsessive. Bowles was turned down for the army when a doctor proclaimed that he had a psychoneurotic personality, and he began to contemplate a career change, perhaps because, as the composer Virgil Thomson said, he realized his lack of formal education would curb his ability to write large-scale works – or perhaps because, as Bowles himself noted, he was excited and thrilled by watching Jane write her novel, *Two Serious Ladies*. In any event he dreamed of Tangier, which he had visited in the 1930s; he regarded it as his magic place, and decided to go there to write a book.

Bowles has published comparatively little: four novels, a handful of story collections, an autobiography, a couple of travel memoirs. His output is uneven and much of it is repetitive in feel and tone. But two books stand out. These are the first story collection, *The Delicate Prey* (a very Bowlesian title, that), and the first novel, *The Sheltering Sky*. Here Bowles seems to be writing ice-cold with a razor, cutting to the bone, laying bare the fragile nature of the civilized instincts. *The Sheltering Sky* describes the processes between and within two American travellers which take them to moral collapse and violent destruction in the Sahara.

Jane followed Bowles to Morocco, and the psychological tension which exists between man and wife in *The Sheltering Sky* had a genesis in reality. Jane knew that in Morocco they were on an unequal footing. Bowles was on his spiritual home turf, taking large quantities of *majoun*, a cannabis jam, to help his writing. *The Sheltering Sky* was a critical and commercial success, selling 40,000 copies in America and funding further travel.

Then it was back to Morocco, where Jane felt unable to write and was never really at ease and where she drank herself into a stroke (there was a rumour that she was poisoned by a lover). He later said: 'I did not know it, but the good years were over.'

Bowles published more books, and devotedly helped Jane during years of steady and tragic decline. She died in 1973, soon after the publication of his autobiography. Bowles has remained in Morocco almost exclusively since her death writing stories and making translations from Arabic.

The story is a fascinating one and Paul Bowles is one of the more remarkable American writers of the postwar period.

Edouard Roditi

Sixty Years of Friendship with Paul Bowles

When Paul Bowles first called on Gertrude Stein, without any previous announcement, in Paris in April 1929, he still signed all his mail and his few published poems with his full name, Paul Frederic Bowles. But the future wartime personal protégée of Marshal Pétain in German-occupied France felt that there was nothing very apostolic about Paul's manner to remind her of the saint of the same name. Instinctively, Gertrude Stein decided then and there that Freddie suited Paul better as a given name, and she and Alice Toklas soon agreed that Freddie had all the characteristics of 'a manufactured savage'.

Paul's education, whether at home or in school, had certainly lacked much that might have led him later to display the main characteristics of a traditional upper-class young man of culture. He appeared indeed to have systematically ignored almost every attempt to educate him. An autodidact by nature, he limited his acquisition of knowledge mainly to what happened to be offered him in order to supply his material needs and what he found in his voracious but still haphazard readings of avant-garde periodicals. All this already made him a striking example of what Paul Goodman, a few decades later, in his best seller entitled *Growing Up Absurd*, accused American education of producing wholesale. In a way, Paul was thus, in 1929, well ahead of his times. By studiously avoiding, later throughout his life, too many and too close contacts with the mass of his American compatriots, Paul finally acquired in Tangier the sophistication and the manner of what Gertrude Stein might now have called 'a manufactured gentleman'.

Unlike Gertrude, I had been corresponding with Paul for quite a while and fairly extensively before we were finally able to meet. Postmarked 3 February 1931, Paul's first postcard to me from New York stated only: 'This I am writing you because there is a chance that we shall meet and because I have enjoyed your poems in *Tambour* and other magazines. I think it a bit necessary that I see you sometime. There are so many worthless people.' Before arriving in Paris, Paul also sent me, in an undated letter, the typescripts of a few of his unpublished poems. When Black Sparrow Press decided many decades later to publish a volume of Paul's early poems, the only known copies of some of those that remained unpublished were still preserved in my personal archives, together with all the letters he ever wrote me. Paul decided, however, that a few of these early unpublished poems were no longer worthy of publication. These are now kept in the Library of the University of California at Los Angeles.

When Paul arrived in Paris as announced in his first postcard from New York, I happened to be studying German in Hamburg, and when he in turn went to Berlin with Aaron Copland, I was already living for a while in London. Several of Paul's letters and postcards express his frustration at failing to meet me anywhere in Europe, or else reflect his amusement when each one of the friends to whom I recommended him in Paris or Berlin described me in turn in such very different terms. In one of his letters, Paul reduced the multiple facets of my rumoured personality to two contradictory characters, one of whom 'should be killed', as if I were some kind of vampire.

In the Paris community of expatriate Americans, it appears from Paul's letters that we had a couple of acquaintances in common before we actually met. These would have been, in particular, Richard Thoma, the editor of *The New Review*, through whom Paul met briefly both Ezra Pound and Jean Cocteau; also Harold Salemson, the editor of *Tambour*, and Eugene Jolas, the editor of *transition*, to which both Paul and I had been, since 1928, the very youngest contributors. Because Paul complained to me so piteously about his material problems in Paris, I recommended him to my friend Carlo Suares, the Egyptian-born, French-language writer and editor of *Cahiers de l'Étoile*, a monthly theosophical journal devoted mainly to propagating the somewhat dissident ideology of Krishnamurti. Very kindly, Suares invited Paul to stay in his apartment, where Paul, according to his host, was no more trouble than a kitten, content to play with the children, to sleep on the living-room sofa and to feed mainly on milk.

While he was still living in Paris, Paul wrote me: 'I am starting again to write stories, and I think you would like them as well as my poems. They are certainly not what Gertrude Stein wants and I think I shall later have to do what she wants because she knows what is good for me and everything else I dare say is easier and I am lazy.' In the long run Gertrude Stein may well have exerted on Paul's prose style a more chastening and lasting effect than on that of Ernest Hemingway. Paul has never lapsed into the kind of absurdly florid imitation of a foreign language that now makes much of *For Whom the Bell Tolls* almost unreadable.

In another letter, Paul reports that Modern Editions in New York was expressing some interest in publishing a few of his poems, but he was very sceptical about this project and confessed that 'they can't be such idiots as to use any of them anyway. I can't be a poet because I'm so sure my stuff is unimportant. I must be a musician because although I'm not believing my music is important I'm not convinced it would necessarily remain unimportant. I might be a painter some day'.

In Paris, Paul was indeed studying musical composition, on Aaron Copland's and Virgil Thomson's recommendation, under Nadia Boulanger, but in several of his letters of 1931 and 1932 he also sent me a few of his drawings. Preserved in the Library of the University of California, these drawings are all strictly surrealist and, however hasty, not ungifted. Some of them even suggest a certainly unconscious affinity with the work of the Czech surrealist painter Josef Sima, who was living in Paris and occasionally contributing illustrations to issues of *Le Grand Jeu*, a dissident surrealist periodical published by a group of Sima's younger French friends which included René Daumal, who was briefly associating at that time with Carlo Suares. Other drawings by Paul now remind me somehow of the early and more overtly surrealist work of Brion Gysin, with whom Paul was not yet acquainted. In many ways, Paul has remained throughout his life a frustrated painter, encouraging others to paint in his stead and exerting in Tangier a profound influence on a few younger Moroccan artists who began to paint and exhibit under his guidance. Of these, the most outstanding remains Driss Yacoubi, who left Tangier to live in New York, where he died.

After a while, Paul decided to accompany Copland to Berlin, where I again recommended him, without having yet met him, to a few of my friends. I was then in London and, in May 1931, he sent me a postcard from Berlin: 'When a few days ago I called on Miss Ross, she introduced me to Sherwood I believe he is called, and to a Polish friend who was staying with her. Sherwood showed me a passport photo of you which makes you look slightly uncanny, or have you mad eyes?' Sherwood, of course, was not the American author of *The Petrified Forest* who later distinguished himself politically as one of the co-authors of President Roosevelt's speeches, but Christopher Isherwood; and Jean Ross, on first meeting Paul that afternoon in Berlin, could hardly have suspected that she would later become famous in literature, in musical comedy and in a movie as Sally Bowles, thanks to Christopher Isherwood. It is surprising that the only evidence of this meeting of Paul and Christopher in Berlin that appears in the published writings of either of them should be Isherwood's borrowing of Paul's name for the most widely known of his fictional female characters, the ultimate heroine of the popular film *Cabaret*, adapted from his Berlin stories.

In one of his letters from Berlin, Paul reported to me at length on 9 June that he had just returned from a trip to Hanover, 'where I have been with Kurt Schwitters setting, or rather translating his vocal sonata into piano music. It was rather fascinating work, the little I did. I had time to do only one scherzo. Have you read much of his stuff? Its importance is rather past, but I still think it has some merits that are at least fun. He as a person is quite mad, but one wonders occasionally if correctly so'.

Not a word of description here of the now legendary Merz Haus where Schwitters lived and which was later destroyed by Allied bombing while Schwitters himself was in wartime exile in England after his perilous escape from Nazi-invaded Norway. From Hanover, Paul returned to Berlin and the rest of this letter is devoted mainly to his reactions to the descriptions of me gathered from my various Berlin friends:

> It is amusing and mysterious to go about hearing of you from one person, then from another. I have a feeling that you are primarily two people, one of which should be killed. Only the Suares version of you should be left living. Not that the others do not give what they consider highly complimentary accounts of you; they do, but for me, only what Suares tells me of you interests me. You see, the others, Jean Ross, Isherwood, von

Braun, even Thoma, all speak of you as clever and witty and amusing, and in the back of it all there is the heavy shadow of nothingness, indecision, unhappiness. Suares says less brilliant things, but there seems in what he says a comprehension which quite outweighs everything the others say. I goad everyone on into talking about you for hours. (All Renée Sintenis said was that your skin was dark and that she was of the opinion that you really hailed from South America.) And they all seem willing to do the talking, on and on; von Braun insists that you are mad. He, by the way, seems extremely hard of understanding. No matter what I say, he says: I don't understand you. It begins to be a sort of song. However he is pleasant, and seems to enjoy being flabbergasted, so it is all right. Only I had always had the idea that I spoke as simply as anyone going. With him, the mind works cautiously like an animal at bay, and we disagree on whatever he does think he understands. *Mais on va.* Jean Ross is of a sort of motherly attitude towards you which is nice.

I had indeed recommended Paul to Jean Ross, the eminent expressionist sculptress Renée Sintenis, and Sigismund von Braun, who was destined, after 1945, to become one of the Federal Republic of Germany's most successful and popular ambassadors, to the United Nations in New York and later to France. Renée Sintenis, by the way, was not the first person, in those years, to suggest that I looked more Latin American than like one of Paul's compatriots. When I met Federico Garcia Lorca briefly two years earlier, in June 1929 in Paris, our Spanish host that evening, the painter Gregorio Prieto, remarked that I truly looked as if I might be Lorca's younger brother. As for my friend Sigismund von Braun, he always tended to express very conventional or conformist opinions, to such an extent that he was even able to serve several years in Hitler's diplomatic corps before finally seeing the light, absconding from his post in Addis Ababa, and seeking refuge in the Vatican City. With Paul, he certainly shared no interests and, some thirty years later, he couldn't remember ever having met him. In his brief reference to the motherly kindness of Jean Ross, Paul proves moreover to have understood her far better than Christopher Isherwood, who was still too provincial a young Englishman to realize that an English girl who happened to have been brought up in

Egypt and able to speak fluent French was not necessarily as promiscuous in her sexual life as his fictional Sally Bowles. Only on the subject of Kurt Schwitters might this letter of Paul's be misleading: the great man of the German Dada movement had good reasons, throughout the years of the Weimar Republic, to stress his political, social and cultural dissidence by deliberately appearing to be insane, though without being at all mad.

But many of these early letters and postcards that Paul was then writing me already display the interest in madness or at least in apparently abnormal behaviour that later surfaces again and again in so many of the characters of his fiction. He had already noted, in one letter, that I appeared in a passport photograph to have mad eyes. Of all the descriptions of my personality that he managed to glean from my various friends, only those that reveal the more outlandish aspects of my character or my life seemed to appeal to him. Yet he also sensed, with unusual insight since he had never yet met me, that all that is clever, witty and amusing in me might well conceal 'the heavy shadow of nothingness, indecision, unhappiness'. This continued indeed to haunt me for many more years, in fact until an electroencephalogram, a relatively novel invention, finally revealed, in the course of a hospitalization for a very different ailment, that I had been mildly epileptic since birth and, as such, subject to frequent accesses of *petit mal*. In Schwitters, too, Paul was fascinated by the streak of feigned insanity that characterizes his Dadaism.

Throughout his stay in Germany, whether in Berlin or in Hanover, Paul appears to have been more concerned with music than with writing or art, since the same long letter, partly quoted above, ends with a hint of his despairing indecision as a younger American composer: 'Aaron Copland is hoping to see you when he goes to London next month. I hope you will be there. He is a swell person. Me, I am stuck here in Berlin while he is in Paris enjoying himself. Ah me, ah me.' After which brief but characteristic expression of self-pity, Paul goes on to complain: 'Music is so difficult. One follows in the footsteps ten years behind, of Antheil, Copland, Blitzstein, twenty behind Hindemith, thirty behind Stravinsky, who said: "*Les autres, ils sont encore romantiques. Moi, je suis déjà romantique.*" Is that right to say or not? I have not decided.' It is interesting to note that Paul fails to mention Virgil Thomson here among his immediate American predecessors, or

Schoenberg or any other major modern composer of the older generation of Hindemith and Stravinsky. Nor does he appear to have become at all aware, while in Berlin, of the new school of *Gebrauchsmusik* represented by Kurt Weil, Ernst Krenek and Eisler, among others.

In another letter from Berlin, Paul returns to the theme of his arguments with Sigismund von Braun, who 'will discuss you, but thinks nothing complimentary of your poems, which subject I feel it is useless for us to argue upon, so I say I haven't read them. Oh, really, they're utter rot, he will tell me, and he writes them in trances, which is even more ridiculous. . . .' Sigismund thus appears to have had, in his twenties, little respect for the trancelike states of rhapsodic poets once described by Plato and Horace and of which, in German literature, some of the poems of Novalis, Hölderlin and even Rilke are such magnificent examples. But Sigismund, in his successful diplomatic career, was fortunately never destined to be a cultural attaché in any German embassy.

In one of my letters to Paul I must have described a dream in which he appeared to me in spite of our having still failed to meet. In reply he wrote: 'I have never dreamed of you, to be sure, and that is a blessing. The fewer people one has to dream about, the less complex life is. And then after I have met you, I shall have you to worry about as well as all the others.' From such an admission, a psychoanalyst might draw eloquent conclusions about the egocentric or narcissistic nature of Paul's emotional life, in which he has so often tended to view himself as the victim of the 'vampirism' of others.

In another undated letter, presumably also of 1931, he refers briefly to his Paris meetings with Ezra Pound and Jean Cocteau, both of whom discussed in his presence and at great length their enthusiasm for talking movies, which were then a great novelty. To me, Paul admitted here that, far from sharing Pound's and Cocteau's enthusiasm, he already regretted the passing of the older silent movies and felt a profound nostalgia for the kind of routine piano music that used to be played in most theatres to accompany them. In more recent years, I have never heard Paul express much interest in any movies except a few silent classics.

When Paul and I finally met, on the occasion of a concert that he had come to London to attend, I was dazzled, like St Gregory in the slave-market of ancient Rome, by the angelic Anglo-Saxon

113

quality of Paul's physical appearance, but soon appalled too by his apparent other-worldliness, helplessness and poverty. It took me some time to realize how deliberately, though perhaps unconsciously, he played the part of the starry-eyed and unmaterialistic young genius, all the better to foist on to others the responsibility of solving in his stead most of his own material problems. For a while, I tried to assume this responsibility and, being unable to cope with his problems with my own financial means, I set about diligently to seek wealthier friends who might support him while enjoying his companionship. In January 1932 Paul thus found a temporary home again in the Paris apartment of my friend Carlo Suares, where he soon had occasion to meet Krishnamurti, the failed rather than false Messiah of the dissident Theosophists.

Although Suares was quite willing to continue supplying Paul with a living-room day-bed and his other modest needs, Paul was becoming restless as a kind of household pet and tempted to travel further afield. Gertrude Stein, I believe, was the first to arouse his interest in Morocco, where she and Alice Toklas had travelled some years earlier, and I too was able to offer him a few superficial descriptions of Tangier, where I had spent a couple of days in 1929 in the course of a Mediterranean cruise with my parents aboard a German Hapag liner. Paul's first trip to Morocco thus took place in 1931 on Gertrude Stein's advice and in the company of Aaron Copland, who was appalled by almost everything he experienced there, while Paul was enchanted. On Paul's return, I was almost miraculously able to scare up successively and within a few months two wealthy and lonely friends, the son of an Australian piano manufacturer and a New York literary agent, one of whom proved willing, in the spring of 1932, to take Paul back to Morocco, while the other, I believe, took him on a tour of Spain. Ultimately, Paul quarrelled with both of them, convinced that they sought somehow to victimize him. In the course of his first visit to Morocco with Aaron Copland, Paul had also been met there, if I remember right, by a wealthy young American friend, Harry Dunham, in whose company he later returned to Morocco.

From this last expedition, Paul and Harry brought back to Paris an impish young Moroccan manservant named Abdelkader who, in the furnished apartment they now occupied with Harry's spinsterly sister Amelia, tried to get to bed with every one of their guests in turn, whether male or female and of whatever age and appearance.

It took Amelia Dunham quite a while to realize what Abdelkader was up to, after which she hastily palmed him off on one of Harry's French friends, who seemed only too glad to satisfy Abdelkader's ever-ready sexual appetite. Some years later I realized, after becoming acquainted in Chicago with American painting of the realist-regionalist school, that Amelia Dunham looked as if she might have posed for the farmer's wife in Grant Wood's immensely popular and slightly caricatural *American Gothic*.

Charles Henri Ford, who had been editing in his home town in the Deep South a little magazine, *Blues*, to which both Paul and I contributed, now also turned up in Paris, a perfect and very conscious example of legendary Southern charm. Paul, Charles Henri and I were then, I believe, the three youngest American poets to be contributing from Paris to a number of expatriate periodicals in Europe as well as to a few avant-garde magazines in America, while also claiming to be the only American representatives of surrealism in poetry, with the possible exception of Harry Crosby and of Eugene Jolas, the much older editor of *transition*, to which we all three managed to contribute from time to time.

Charles Henri was very proud of being the co-author, with Parker Tyler, another young Southern avant-garde poet, of *The Young and Evil*, a novel that has become a classic of experimental American fiction of that era rather than, as he claims erroneously, the first American homosexual novel, which was probably *Belchamber*, by Howard Sturges, a friend of Henry James. In Paris, Charles Henri now managed to become a favoured member of Gertrude Stein's 'charmed circle' of admiring younger writers and artists, and to be admitted also into the equally exclusive and utterly charmed circle of Jean Cocteau. It was presumably at the court of Gertrude Stein that Charles Henri originally met the painter Pavel Tchelitchew, in whose life and affections he soon replaced the less glamorous and more timorous American pianist Alan Tanner.

To his new Paris friends, Charles needed to provide proof that he was indeed as evil as he was still young. He therefore decided to set about exploring some of the sinks of sheer iniquity for which the French capital had long been famous. Having heard that its Turkish baths deserved, as such, to be explored, he hesitated to visit any of them alone, perhaps because of his inability to express himself fluently in French. Of his various Paris friends, he began first to

115

inquire which baths might be most worth visiting. Because both Virgil Thomson and the painter Maurice Grosser proved quite properly to be unwilling to lead such a youngster as Charles astray by giving him the address of any of these baths, Charles commissioned me, if only as a suitable guide because of my fluency in French, to inquire among my own French friends which establishments might be well worth our visiting together. Several such baths were recommended to me by the painter Christian Bérard, the film actor Roland Caillaud, who later illustrated the first edition of the poems of Jean Genet, and a couple of other friends. After much hesitation, Charles finally convinced Paul to accompany him, with me as their Virgil, on their infernal expedition, and the three of us then went together, one weekday afternoon, to the baths on the Rue Desmoines, a small street near the Place Clichy.

This 'Temple of Indecency', as the owner of another such establishment, the real-life model for Proust's Jupien, would prudishly have called it, was almost deserted when we arrived there, hospitably greeted by its whole idle staff of pale and pasty-faced young masseurs. These promptly offered us their services, which we refrained from accepting. Two or three older types soon began also to hover around us hesitantly and none too hopefully. Suddenly, a handsome young Arab followed us into the steam-room and first tried his luck with Paul, the only one of us who was fair-haired. Like a nymph pursued by a lusty satyr in a mannerist Italian painting, Paul fled in a panic to the relative safety of the lounge. Many years later he admitted to me that he could remember, of this whole afternoon, only that he had been 'in acute anguish throughout the episode'.

Rejected by Paul, the young Arab then turned his attention to Charles, only to be repulsed as firmly, though not as fearfully, as by Paul. Assuming that I, because of my Mediterranean physical appearance, might happen to be a compatriot, he began chatting innocently enough with me, expressing some surprise at being treated in so unfriendly a manner by my two companions. After all, why were we all four here? He seemed to be a nice enough guy and, after a while, we retired together to one of the private rooms, where he proved to be a truly delightful partner.

In the eyes of both Charles Henri and Paul, I thus revealed myself as more evil than either of them, though still as young, and my new Arab friend later tried to date me for the following week, but I was still too class-conscious or race-conscious to become involved in a closer relationship of this kind in Paris, where I was still living with my parents. Nor did I ever, in all the ensuing decades, return to the baths of the Rue Desmoines.

In the same file as all of Paul's early letters to me and as the poems and drawings enclosed in some of these, I now find also a clipping of an article, signed I.M.P., that was published at some time in those years in a New York daily:

Paul Frederic Bowles sends us scraps of news from that dear Paris. . . . 'Edouard Roditi, one of the standbys of *transition*, is going to start a magazine. The interesting thing about this one is that it is anti-literary. He is going to limit its contributors considerably by including a large percentage of manuscripts from schizophrenics, dipsomaniacs, various mystics and other enemies of literature and society in general. . . . *The New Review*, which Samuel Putnam, Ezra Pound and Richard Thoma are editing there, brings out its second number this week. They gave a dinner last week for Pound and Cocteau. . . . I had tea at Gertrude Stein's a few days ago. She is getting out a new edition of "all the work not yet printed" of Gertrude Stein. After *Lucy Church Amiably, a Novel of Romantic Beauty and which looks like an engraving*, she promises the new *How to write* series. I think perhaps it will be one of the most important of her books. Nancy Cunard is on the Côte d'Azur and is giving up publishing for a while, as it bores her, so I suppose we will have no more Hours Press books. . . . Jean Cocteau told me he enjoys the talkies more than the silent, and that it is stupid to whine for the old ones. . . . Well, is the Chrysler Building all finished?'

Most of the gossip here attributed to Paul and reprinted in a New York daily newspaper also appears in some of his letters to me, in several of which he likewise refers at some length to my alleged project of a new periodical, of which I have no recollection and, in my archives, no other written proof. I can only surmise now that I was encouraged, by my interest in Professor Prinzhorn's pioneer German study, *Bildnerei der Geisteskranken*, on the art of the insane, to suggest that a similar study of the writings of schizophrenics and other mental patients would be of equal interest, and that

Paul, with his lifelong interest in the irrational, then assumed that I somehow intended to undertake this task on my own.

Many years later, my New York friend Henrietta von Westphalen pointed out to me that the probable source of the rumour reported in this article so mysteriously by I.M.P. may well have been the writer Samuel Putnam, one of the editors of *The New Review*. In his book of memoirs entitled *Paris Was Our Mistress* one finds the following remark, which he claims I made to him, not to Paul: 'Edouard Roditi, at that time a contributor to *transition*, now a well-known American scholar, announced with tongue in cheek his intention of founding a magazine whose contributors would be limited to dipsomaniacs, dope fiends, schizophrenics, and Hindu mystics.' I was well ahead, it seems, of my time. In recent years, such periodicals have almost become a commonplace.

After his return from Paris to America, I ceased for a long while to maintain contact with Paul, until we met again in New York during the Second World War, again as contributors to the same periodical, this time to *View*, edited by Charles Henri Ford. On my return to Europe in 1946 my only contact with Paul, for many years, was my publication of a German translation of one of his stories in Berlin in *Das Lot*, of which I was one of the editors.

In 1960 I returned to Tangier for the first time since 1929, soon purchased a house there, and thus began to see Paul and Jane fairly regularly for several months every summer. It was even at one time my intention to retire later to Tangier. But the city began, in the following ten years, gradually to lose much of its charm in my eyes. Its native Italian, Spanish and Jewish population was emigrating, while many of its older French, English or American residents either died or moved elsewhere. Morocco's demographic explosion and ensuing pauperization were also transforming the city's colourful old Medina and many of its outlying districts into a tangle of slums. With the impending threat of the ever more imminent closing down of the American Consulate, I decided, unlike Paul, that Tangier might soon cease to be the ideal place for an American writer to spend his old age, and I therefore sold my house.

For about ten years I refrained from returning to Tangier, but kept in regular contact with Paul by mail. Late in 1990 I returned briefly to Morocco and stopped for a few days in Tangier to visit him. I was shocked by the deterioration in his health, but gratified to find him surrounded by a small court of faithful admirers and well-wishers. Memories of my earlier encounters with him as the 'manufactured savage' described by Gertrude Stein reveal my own surprised reactions of sixty years earlier to a new kind of American youth who was then novel to both Gertrude Stein and me as American expatriates of long standing. Now these memories make me wonder what mysterious *Letters to a Young Man Whose Education Has Been Neglected*, similar to those that Thomas de Quincey once wrote to his anonymous and probably fictitious correspondent, have gradually managed to transform Paul Bowles into the 'manufactured gentleman' and dignified elder statesman of American letters who enchants the many pilgrims flocking to his Tangier apartment as if it were already one of the more hallowed shrines of American literature.

Should we already begin to collect funds in order to purchase the Itesa building in Tangier, where both Paul and Jane Bowles lived for so many years, and then maintain it for posterity, much as the homes of Edgar Allan Poe or Emily Dickinson are already preserved in America?

Ned Rorem

A Note on Paul Bowles

Since we first met a half-century ago in Taxco, not a day has passed without my thinking of Paul Bowles. The thinking involves mainly his music. I was a vacationing music student, age seventeen, and Paul was, at thirty, a professional composer. Indeed, he was the first professional I'd ever known, and I loved his music. He played me a great deal of it during that July of 1941; I was bewitched and never recovered. Would Paul enjoy comparing my situation to that of Lord Henry Wotton (in Wilde's famous novel), who lends Dorian Gray a copy of Huysmans's *A Rebours*, precipitating poor Dorian's descent into 'aesthetic corruption'? Alas, Paul's music is the picture of healthiness. A more proper analogy might be the *petite phrase* of Proust's musician, Vinteuil, which so coloured the hero's life.

The *petite phrase* in this case was that most melancholy of intervals, a descending minor third, the 'dying fall' that threads Paul's music from the early 1940s. Listen again to the songs on Lorca texts, or to the crowning aria in *The Wind Remains*, his little zarzuela based on a Lorca play. The phrase is a mannerism of which Paul is doubtless unaware: we live with our signatures, after all, so never think much about them. For me, though, it was a conscious expressive device which I appropriated and have retained to this day.

In the intervening decades I have probably composed ten times more music than has Paul (with the 1949 advent of *The Sheltering Sky* he moved, in the ken of the general public, from the role of composer-who-also-writes to that of author-who-used-to-compose), yet not one piece is without the rhythmic or melodic lilt, albeit disguised, of the invisible mentor. (Thus in my guilt, not a day has passed, etc.) Influence, of course, is what all art stems from: thievery is embellished, then stamped – often for the worse – with the new owner's tic.

Paul and I are separated enough in years for me still to wish, at sixty-seven, for his approval. He would certainly profess astonishment at this juvenile admission, especially since he probably wouldn't see – or hear – himself in me. But I am thrilled to give him credit here.

If I stress Paul's musicality, it's because that musicality seems to have fallen away in our world. The bulk of his fans are unaware that he ever composed, much less have they ever hummed his tunes: Americans are meant to be specialists. So for the record let it be said that Paul Bowles is, like great Europeans of yore (Leonardo, Cocteau, Noël Coward), a general practitioner of a high order. Unlike them, his two professions don't overlap – either aesthetically or technically. Composers when they prosify (Schumann, Debussy, Thomson), inevitably deal with music or with autobiography. Bowles is the sole fiction writer among them, and his fiction is as remote from their prose as from his own music. His books are icy, cruel, objective, moralistic in their inexorable amorality, and occurring mostly in exotic climes; they are also often cast in large forms. His music is warm, wistful, witty and redolent of nostalgia for his Yankee youth; it wears its heart on its sleeve, and is all cast in small forms.

No American in our century has composed songs lovelier than Paul Bowles's. None of these songs is currently available in print. That fact, in its way, echoes the indifferent world that he elsewhere so successfully portrays.

John Ryle

A Refuge in the Shadows of the Tangier Casbah

In Tangier, in the Casbah, the narrow streets are blocked with sandbags. Bullet holes are etched in pristine white walls: machine-guns stutter in the back alleys. Once the international zone of Morocco, now a decayed Mediterranean seaside town, Tangier is back in fashion – this time as a film set. On wrought-iron balconies the cameras roll. The Casbah stands in for some other oriental town, or impersonates itself in former days – when Tangier was the Lotus-land of the post-war Bohemian diaspora, a refuge for rich and sexually eccentric Westerners: or when, a decade later, it became a beat shrine, a hippie haven, boarding-point for the Marrakesh Express.

Today they are filming the battle of Beirut; one day soon, *The Naked Lunch*, the beat burlesque that Burroughs cut up and pasted together in a hotel in Tangier in the early 1950s. But the major project of the current shooting season has been *The Sheltering Sky*, Bertolucci's film of the odd, haunting book written – some years before *The Naked Lunch* – by Tangier's most celebrated foreign resident, the American composer, writer and translator, Paul Bowles.

The Sheltering Sky, Bowles's first novel, published in 1949, is the story of an American couple who wander down into the Sahara from the coast of North Africa. Troubled in spirit, enmeshed in a culture older and tougher than their own, they fall apart, go mad and die. It is a theme that recurs in Bowles's work: many of his stories are of hapless Europeans or Americans – Nazarenes (Bowles's translation of the Maghrebi Arabic word for Christian, meaning any Westerners) – who venture too deep into societies that are not their own. 'They are ants,' he has said of the indigenous inhabitants of such countries. 'We are their aphids.'

Today, when Islam presses closer on the citadels of the West, his tales have a special interest. Are these chilling narratives part of a tradition of orientalist fantasy? Or does Bowles have a more distinctive claim as chronicler of the cultural divide?

Bowles was born in Queens, New York, in 1910. But he is the most un-American of authors. None of his four novels is set in America, and very few of his short stories. In his youth he was taken up by Gertrude Stein and introduced to the modernist crew in Paris, and his deepest affinities are with writers of the European tradition – with Kafka and Borges and Beckett. His one native influence is the father of American gothic, Edgar Allan Poe.

After the war he led a peripatetic life with his wife, Jane, a writer of similarly quirky reputation, living for some years in Central America and South Asia. Finally in the late 1940s they settled in Tangier, Tangier of the international zone, the *louche* Tangier of Barbara Hutton, the Woolworth heiress, lure for the hip and the homosexual and the culturally centrifugal.

Bowles still lives here, in the same nondescript apartment block, a mile or so from the Casbah, that they moved into over thirty years ago. Jane Bowles died from a stroke in 1973. Now in his eightieth year, Bowles is looked after by his driver, Abdelouahaid Boulaich, and by one of his Moroccan protégés, Mohammed Mrabet. He has taped and translated from the Arabic a dozen books of Mrabet's stories, almost as many as he has published himself.

The publication of Bowles's journal of his life in Morocco comes as something of a surprise: he is a noticeably reticent writer. His autobiography, *Without Stopping*, published in 1972, is elegant but unrevealing. He is probably the only autobiographer whose friends have complained of his lack of indiscretion. William Burroughs called it *Without Telling*. Even Gore Vidal – one of Bowles's most consistent admirers – said you had to read between the lines.

The journal is altogether thinner – there are not many lines to read between – and its most animated passages are where Bowles wrinkles his nose at his biographer, Christopher Sawyer-Laucanno, whose unwelcome attentions resulted in a biography, *An Invisible Spectator*, published in 1989. It seems possible that Sawyer-Laucanno failed to perceive how much his subject resented his questions – Bowles acknowledges this possibility in his journal – but future interviewers are left in no doubt as to the thin ice they walk on.

As we wait for Bowles outside his apartment, shiny new BMWs and Mercedes, shipped in by Moroccan *Gastarbeiter* on their return from Europe, criss-cross in the street. From the traffic emerges a distinctive vehicle – Bowles's vintage Ford Mustang, caramel-coloured, with wild horses moulded in relief on the grey leather seats. Out of it steps Bowles, not without difficulty – he is recovering from an attack of sciatica – but with perfectly coiffed white hair and immaculate clothes: pale buckskin jacket, fawn Dunhill sweater, tan-coloured permanent-press trousers and polished shoes.

Since the 1960s, when he became required reading on the hippie trail, along with Ginsberg and Kerouac, young admirers have made their way to Bowles's apartment expecting to meet a raddled Buddha, an ageing beatnik sage. Instead they are confronted with this vision of button-down elegance. They do not know, perhaps, that in the 1930s Paul Bowles was the toast of Bohemian Europe – one of his suitors professing himself struck 'like St Gregory in the slave-market' by his blond good looks. Now, in his final years, he is *senex florescans*, dapper and radiant.

We accompany him and Abdelouahaid up to the apartment, carrying a huge bunch of flowers he has been given by Gavin Young, an occasional resident of Tangier, with whom he has been having lunch. The living-room of the apartment is dark, the curtains drawn, the fire set in the grate. The only light is filtered through a dense mass of dusty green plants on the terrace. The books in the shelves are darkened by soot and flame, giving them a Gothic hue. The titles seem to fit: *Midnight Mass*, *The Delicate Prey*, *The Spider's House*, *She Woke Me Up so I Killed Her*. We sit, Moroccan-style, amid cushions on low divans, drinking tea. I ask Bowles if he writes here.

'No,' he says. 'As a matter of fact, I write in bed. I got into the habit in the desert. It was cold there at night, extremely cold – there would be ice in the water-jar by morning. The only place where you could keep your writing hand warm was under the blanket. I find if I write at a desk I jump up every fifteen minutes.'

Bowles writes in a tiny truckle bed in the corner of a room piled with dusty tapes of his musical compositions, and recordings made many years ago on ethnomusicological expeditions to the interior of Morocco. There is an unused synthesizer keyboard in the bedroom, a cassette deck and a supper-tray – these days he also eats in bed.

In his study, the last room in the apartment, the curtains are open and the afternoon sun pours in. This is the only room with a chair. There is a wardrobe with silk ties poking from the half-closed door: books in French and English are piled on the floor. Where the books in the living-room are scorched by fire, the books in the study are faded by the sun. From the window of the study you can see the Dradeb quarter, houses cascading down the hillside like tumbling dice: beyond them, the Old Mountain, where the last of the rich expatriates live.

The bookshelves in the apartment are dotted with figurines, tiny mementoes thick with dust, some rare and exquisite, some tawdry or kitsch. There are no large objects: the biggest things are books. In the hallway is a stack of leather suitcases: they, too, are layered with dust. Bowles never leaves Tangier. Or hardly ever: he went to Paris in 1988 and regretted it. It is more than a quarter of a century since he visited America. 'I haven't enjoyed travelling since ships went out of style,' he says. 'Jane and I always went by ship. We didn't travel light – we had two trunks and about twenty valises. That's why I'm here in Tangier. This is where I was when ships with passengers were taken off the surface of the sea.'

I ask him if the making of the film of *The Sheltering Sky* showed him anything in the book he wasn't already aware of. 'I can't say it did,' he laughs. 'And I sold the rights years ago, so I make no money from it. . . .'

What about his part in the film?

'It's a very little one. I'm just a figure in the background, though I did get to spend a few days on the set.'

Did he enjoy it?

'It would be an exaggeration to say I did. I just sat there thinking: My protagonists, *there they go*. . . . The amazing thing about the film was the way they rebuilt Tangier as Oran. They even put down rails for streetcars. The Moroccans here had never seen a streetcar. They thought it was something very modern. To make it more authentic they set out to remove every single piece of plastic from the city. Even from the city dump – imagine! So Debra Winger could walk through pristine garbage. . . . Then they dressed everyone in rags. They paid someone to put rips and tears in all the burnous. They looked terrible. Actually, as I remember, people looked much better in 1947 than they do today.'

Japanese kodo music is playing in the room. 'They are threatening to use this for the sound-track of the film,' says Bowles with distaste.

Have they asked his opinion?

'Oh, I don't think they know I do anything other than write books,' he says.

This is false modesty, however. They know – and Bowles must know they know – that he wrote the scores for a dozen films in the 1930s and 1940s. A pupil of Aaron Copland, with whom he first came to Tangier, he earned his living for many years as a composer, writing incidental music for most of Tennessee Williams's plays and for the stage version of *South Pacific*.

To listen to Bowles's music after reading his books is to enter a different world. The mood is one of lightness, with touches of absurdity. Cigar-boxes and milk bottles vie with the conventional instruments of the orchestra. Despite his knowledge of Moroccan folk music, his compositions show hardly any exotic influence. 'That's what people say,' says Bowles, 'that my music has nothing to do with my writing. I don't know whether I'd agree. Quite a few of my pieces are songs that I wrote the words for myself.'

True enough: tender and mildly nonsensical, the lyrics of Bowles's songs are perfectly at ease with the music he puts them to. Virgil Thomson said of them: 'The texts fit the tunes like a peach in its skin.' 'Should be the other way round, really,' says Bowles, with nonchalant precision.

Perhaps one should say, then, that Bowles's prose has a depth and austerity not present in his musical compositions. It is the difference between the shadow world of the living-room and the sunlit study.

There is a link, though, at the level of form. Like Chopin, Bowles is a musical miniaturist. He is also a miniaturist of prose. His most perfect works are not novels but short stories. His best musical pieces are songs and short instrumental works. He agrees.

'My short stories are generally better than my novels. As you say, I am a miniaturist. I don't mind at all having written small things. It's a question of the *desire to be impressive*. That's what wrong with opera, its desire to be impressive. I started making translations when Jane was ill. She lived in the downstairs apartment. There was a telephone between her room and mine and she'd call about every fifteen minutes so I didn't have the isolation or the leisure to sit and invent at length. Now translations and short stories are my chosen form.'

A special penalty of exile for Bowles is that he never hears his work performed live: the last time was in 1948. Tapes and scores gather dust. Many have been lost. The maid, he says, steals the cassettes.

'She likes your music?'

'Oh no. She likes to record over it. Mrabet thinks I should sack her. Of course, he thinks I should also sack Abdelouahaid.'

Bowles seems invigorated by the ill-will between members of his household. It is not, one feels, *schadenfreude* on his part, more a form of existentialism: recognizing the ubiquity of malice makes him merry. There is a telling film-clip of him talking to Mick Jagger in this room a year ago. Jagger, who seems to have done a bit of homework, says to Bowles: 'Er – you're quite pessimistic, aren't you?' Bowles, with a brilliant smile says: 'Yes. I guess I am.'

Mohammed Mrabet plays a special part in Bowles's view of the world. Street-boy and beachcomber, now married with a family, Mrabet is Bowles's long-time collaborator. He comes every evening to light the fire and cook Bowles's dinner. His name is on the spine of dozens of the books on the shelves in the apartment. Yet Mrabet cannot read or write. The books, including several novels and a scabrous autobiography, are all recorded and translated by Bowles.

Mrabet's autobiography, *Look and Move On*, describes, among other things, a brief sojourn in the United States. Picked up by a gay American in Tangier and taken to Iowa, he scandalizes his hosts by killing and cooking robins from the garden in a stew, a *tajine*. A chapter describing a subsequent visit to California is called 'Like The Sahara only Dirty'. *Look and Move On*, despite the resonance in the title, is just the opposite of *Without Stopping*. Where Bowles is mild and discreet, Mrabet is racy and subversive. It seems that Mrabet's literary persona serves as an alter ego for his translator.

Mrabet has a nasty reputation among Bowles's expatriate friends: they tend to roll their eyes at the mention of his name. Bowles's journal records how Mrabet assaulted an American photographer friend because she brought a larger bunch of flowers than he had already provided for the apartment. 'Mrabet', writes Bowles, 'began to bellow that he was in a room full of Jews who should be killed and not allowed to pollute the air breathed by a Muslim . . .

Abdelouahaid sat shaking his head. He whispered: "A horrible man. Heart of tar."'

The sun is setting over the mountain. Perhaps, I reflect, it is time for us to leave. Before we can move, though, we hear the key turn in the front-door lock. 'Here he comes,' says Bowles.

The man who enters the apartment is about fifty, quite small, the same height as Bowles. Bowles introduces us. '*Enchanté*,' says Mrabet. He fills a kif pipe and lights it. Twice, three times. The flaring match illuminates his face. He smiles.

'You are from London?' asks Mrabet. 'Many of my family are there. London is perfect. It's cold. It rains. The police are kind. Let's talk about London. Let's not talk about Tangier.'

We discuss Hyde Park, and the Moroccan community in Kensington. English robins, we decide, are too small to make good *tajine*. I learn that one of Mrabet's novels, *Love with a Few Hairs*, was adapted for television and broadcast by the BBC in the 1970s. Mrabet is genial, positively mellow. Can this be Bowles's Caliban? His Scheherazade? The man with the heart of tar? It must be a good day.

'Mrabet thinks I should charge for interviews,' says Bowles. 'Five hundred dollars a time.' In that case, I say to Mrabet, perhaps he would like to conduct the last part of the interview himself. What is the question he would most like to put to his translator – the five hundred dollar question?

Mrabet answers in Spanish, the language he mainly uses with Bowles. 'I would ask him', he says with a serious air, 'about all the people he has made love to – since I met him.'

Bowles translates. Both of them know that decorum prevents asking any such question. It is Mrabet's way of teasing Bowles – and ending the conversation.

Story-teller and translator, master and servant, Muslim and Nazarene, ant and aphid – it would be something to hear the story of the long and productive collaboration of these two men. The subject is barely touched on in either of their autobiographies. For Mrabet it has produced a body of work almost as substantial as Bowles's own, while for Bowles the act of translation – and the ambiguous dependencies it entails – seems to have saved him from the fate of one of his own characters. Instead of wandering off into the desert, he has earthed himself in other people's stories, burrowing into the host culture, dispersing part of his authorial impulse in the task of bringing the lives of others to light, and others' words to written form.

Maria St Just

I admire Paul Bowles enormously as a writer. He was very good company and I do remember one thing that Tennessee Williams said: 'Paul was always much more interesting than the places he lived in.'

When my youngest daughter, Natasha, went to Tangier ten years ago, I wrote to Paul asking if he would see her. Natasha couldn't find him in the Socco, so Paul very kindly went to Natasha's hotel and found that she had just left. He wrote me a most infuriated and terribly funny letter saying: 'Not only have I not found your beastly daughter, but I have had to pay extra postage on the letter you sent me.'

I think it wonderful that his talent over the years has never diminished and I know that he helped Tennessee enormously with his work and through his beautiful musical compositions. I send him my love and next time I write I shall put more stamps on the letter.

Emilio Sanz de Soto

*Spanish and Latin-American Names in Paul Bowles's World
(translated from the Spanish by James Ray Green)*

If my notes (I don't call them diaries because they aren't exactly diaries), saved in small notebooks throughout the forties and fifties, do not deceive me, I met Paul Bowles for the first time on 6 October 1947 in the Parade bar in Tangier, in its original location in the commercial arcade of the Cortasa Building on Des Vignes Street, opposite the Paris Cinema. José (Pepe) Carleton Abrines was with me, as he always was during those years, and we were both struck by the beauty and elegance of a couple, the proximity of whose table to ours permitted us to hear now that 'she' was discussing with 'him' Rainer Maria Rilke's letters to Princess Marie von Thurn und Taxis.

Never since have I seen in person a face like hers. And I say 'in person' because until that day I had thought that only on the screen, thanks to that marvellous 'lie' which is the cinema, would I ever have been able to contemplate the real unreality of Greta Garbo's face. And yet another face, almost identical, but this one very real in its unreality, was so near me, almost within my reach, a profile, almost motionless, from which phrases emerged in English, with a few German words mixed in, with a harmony which to my ear was perfect in its clarity.

Listening to her was an impeccably dressed young blond man, typically Anglo-Saxon with perhaps a trace of the Germanic, smoking small, strange-smelling cigarettes in one of those cigarette-holders (long forgotten today) that gave smoking a very special ritualistic quality. I am, of course, referring to Paul Bowles, then thirty-seven years old.

Both Pepe Carleton and I were mesmerized by that pair, who produced in us that bewilderment about life and its protagonists which is so typical of twenty-year-olds and which time manages to erode. Only a recollection survives, and with that recollection the recovery of sensations we regarded as lost for ever.

Also there, talking and laughing very audibly, was Jay Hazelwood, barman at the Parade, and also the co-owner, as I remember. Speaking to 'her', he said: 'Here at the bar we are trying to figure out a quiz book devoted to twentieth-century artists and writers, most of them apparently famous, but there are many pitfalls. Imagine it's my lot to guess three great Spanish poets, and all I have are photos of a very respectable-looking bearded gentleman and two rather handsome young men. You can easily see that it's just a trick. Could today's Spain possibly have such distinguished poets?'

To our great surprise, the person who had so captivated our attention answered, and not without a tinge of irritation in her voice: 'My dear Jay, don't be ignorant. Surely the photos you refer to are of Juan Ramón Jiménez, Federico García Lorca and 'Luisito' Cernuda. Bring me the book, and I'll verify it for you at once.' She pronounced the three poets' names in perfect Spanish, whose softened vowels reflected a slight Argentine cadence.

When Jay the bartender took them the book, which had been left in the Parade months before by Thornton Wilder and a young friend of his, a Spanish Jesuit, 'she', after taking a look at it, said quite audibly: 'Paul, who is this?', pointing to one of the photographs. To this Paul responded: 'I only recognize Juan Ramón Jiménez. Obviously neither of the others is Federico García Lorca.'

In the face of such doubt, I could not resist getting up and, without even introducing myself, I looked at the photos and said: 'The "unidentified" poet is none other than Rafael Alberti.' And then I added: 'What surprises me is that you know and recognize Cernuda and that you call him "Luisito".' Response: 'Yes, I met him at a dinner given for us at the Dorchester by the Madariagas. Salvador is a good friend of my husband, Kenneth. Cernuda made a lasting impression on me. His shyness, his nervous twitch, his silences. That night I began to intuit what a great poet he is. I recall that after dinner in the hotel bar we spent awhile talking about one of his favourite topics, Elizabeth Barrett Browning's *Sonnets from the Portuguese*.'

Through the years this singular person has never ceased to surprise and amaze me. Her name: Beatrix Pendar, née Llambí-Campbell. Her father was the Argentine Ambassador in Berlin and also in Paris, I believe.

Paul Bowles and Beatrix Pendar met in New York at the residence of the Marquis of Cuevas, where many Spaniards often got together, among them Salvador Dali, always with Gala in tow, the Spanish dancers Rosario and Antonio, the composer Gustavo Pittaluga and his wife, the actress Ana Maria Custodio, who was besieged by the *amour fou* of Alexander Calder, who gave her jewels he had designed, jewels that were displayed many years later in Clan, the art gallery owned by Tomás Seral y Casas, a friend of Beatrix and Paul, about whom I shall have more to say later.

I have never understood why Paul does not quote Beatrix in his memoirs, *Without Stopping*. They tell me that today Beatrix and Paul send each other *des petits mots*. She is confined in the Italian Hospital in Tangier, an old building on Buarrakia Street, also known to elderly Arabs in the city as 'Cemetery Street'.

I feel I must devote a few paragraphs to Federico García Lorca; for he is, without a doubt, the one figure from among the essential names in contemporary Spanish literature who was to exert the greatest influence on Paul Bowles – or rather, the one who inspired some of Paul's greatest musical works.

As Paul himself acknowledges, it was the Mexican composer Silvestre Revueltas who revealed to him Lorca's poetic grandeur. With a letter of introduction from Aaron Copland for Revueltas, Paul went to the Conservatory in Mexico City – and before he could even introduce himself, he heard the Mexican composer masterfully conduct his *Homenaje a García Lorca*. From that moment on the poet from Granada was read with intense passion by Paul Bowles, who was brilliant in his restless youth and for whom words would always have a musical value.

On one occasion Paul told me that, after learning the elementary rules of Spanish grammar, he actually learned the language by reading the Chilean poet Vicente Huidobro, specifically his *Altazor*, a truly original work in the Hispanic poetic tradition. Those familiar with this book will no doubt be surprised at this, given the poetry's innovative and hermetic language. It's a bit like learning French by reading Arthur Rimbaud or learning English by reading the most recondite passages from Lewis Carroll.

During those years Paul Bowles was a bit uneasy, for he had made a commitment to compose a non-traditional opera. It was precisely then that he discovered Lorca's theatrical work, *Así que pasen cinco años*, a work already imbued with that surrealism with which he wanted to astonish his two 'friends/enemies', namely Salvador Dali and Luis Buñuel. After translating Lorca's work into English, Paul realized how difficult it would be to transform such a broken text into an opera. He said: 'It's rather like a puzzle of dazzling poems', and he finally opted for selecting certain scenes, thereby reducing the action and simultaneously giving the work a lighter tone. But as he proceeded with the score he came to the conclusion that it was not an opera but a zarzuela. It is certainly debatable whether this term is indeed applicable to Paul's work, which would finally be given the title *The Wind Remains*, but the mere fact that a non-Spanish composer should call one of his compositions a zarzuela has undeniable charm. Bowles knew of the enthusiasm Nietzsche expressed for Spain's *género chico* after hearing Chueca's *La Gran Vía* and he felt, not without reason, that if this type of music – so deeply rooted in the Spanish spirit – captivated Nietzsche, then the same thing had happened to him.

The Wind Remains opened on 30 March 1943 at the Museum of Modern Art. Its subtitle was 'Zarzuela Based on Scenes from *Así que pasen cinco años* by Federico García Lorca'.

The work was produced by the Marquise of Casa Fuerte, Leonard Bernstein was in charge of the musical direction and Schyler Watts of the staging. Oliver Smith designed the sets and costumes, Merce Cunningham was the choreographer, and the singers were Jeanne Stephens, soprano, and Rómolo de Spirito, tenor. It was a prestigious success.

In 1958 the American Music Edition of New York produced a recording of four of Lorca's songs for voice and piano, with music by Paul Bowles. It is one of the most beautiful musical creations of this composer, destined to become a novelist. The recording has the Spanish title *Cuatro canciones* and includes the following songs by Lorca: 'Cancioncilla', 'Balada amarilla', 'Media luna' and 'Murió al amanecer'.

That same year finally witnessed the première of Bowles's opera based on Lorca's *Yerma*, a work he had begun in 1947, commissioned by the singer Libby Holman, who was very enthusiastic about Lorca's play. This opera never convinced the New York critics who travelled to the University of Denver to attend the première on 29 July 1958. It should be noted, however, that the critics blamed the opera's weakness not on Bowles's score or on the conducting by the Catalonian Carlos Surinach, whom Bowles always held in high esteem, but rather on Libby Holman's voice, which had undergone a marked decline between 1947 and 1958.

Among the Spanish musicians Paul Bowles met, Manuel de Falla should occupy a privileged first place. In the spring of 1932 he could not resist going to Granada on a secret pilgrimage to meet the author of that 'Retablo de Maese Pedro' which so fascinated him. After asking in the hotel where Falla's house was located and finding out that it was nearby, Paul set out – without thinking twice – for his 'carmen' on the Antequeruela Alta, beneath the Alhambra. And the same thing happened to Paul that happened to all the others. He was astonished that the gentleman he found there, dressed in black, who seemed so frail, so simple, could be the composer of such powerful, such sensual music. It was difficult to believe, but it was so. Aaron Copland said of Falla: 'He is the only motionless reflection among the many that never stop moving both day and night all around the Alhambra.'

Falla seemed determined that Paul should value above all his other works the Concerto for Harpsichord which he had composed for Wanda Landowska. But Paul remained (and remains) devoted to the 'Retablo'. Perhaps he remembers that Pepe Carleton and I brought him from Madrid the recording of the 'Retablo' by Ernesto Halffter, with Lola Rodriguez Aragón. According to the new generation, the very personal voice of Lola Rodriguez Aragón achieves in this work by Falla such a thorough interpenetration of text and music that it will probably never be matched in a recording.

Besides Falla, I am sure Paul met Joaquín Nin, born in Havana, student of the legendary Felipe Pedrell, father of Anaïs Nin, and about whom Falla used to say that, more than composer and pianist he was, wherever he appeared, 'the favourite of the ladies'. Anaïs Nin's novel *The House of Incest* is, according to the author herself, 'the dreamed reality of true events'. Consequently, father and daughter took every possible precaution never to be in the same place at the same time, and apparently they succeeded. Anaïs Nin's husband, who was forced to lead a double life – as a bank employee (Hugh Guiler) and as a film director (Ian Hugo), made from the novel a surrealist film with identical theme and title: *The House of*

Incest. And whenever Luis Buñuel was asked the proverbial (and ridiculous) question about which was the best film and which the worst film ever made, he would answer: 'The best was one I saw at age five, a silent film, and who knows what its title was, and the worst, without a shadow of doubt, *The House of Incest*, which, fortunately, almost no one has seen.'

Paul also met Nin's other son, Anaïs's unacknowledged brother, the composer Joaquín Nin-Culmell, who for many years was professor in various universities in the United States. He is the author of several fine songs based on Spanish themes, and Teresa Berganza generally keeps a few of these songs in her very select repertoire. It was Joaquín Nin-Culmell who told me that Paul had met him and his father, as well as Anaïs. Jane told me that whenever Paul had nightmares, Anaïs would appear before him wrapped in newspaper and with her head shaved.

Another Spanish musician exiled in New York, whose life is a splendid intrigue for many of his contemporaries and whom Paul met, according to Esteban Frances (more about him later), is Gustavo Duran. He was a minor musician, but the author of a few ballets for the greatest Spanish dancer of all time: Antonia Mercé, 'La Argentina'. In 1991 the centenary of 'La Argentina' was celebrated in Madrid's Maria Guerrero Theatre with a perfect evocation of her dances, her costumes, her sets – and I was astonished.

Among the many Spanish-speaking poets, novelists, musicians, and painters whom Paul Bowles knew personally, the largest contingent is the group of painters. Here I shall limit my list to painters from Spain and one from Panama, who has been a friend of both Paul and of mine for many years. At the top of the list, without any doubt, is the name of Salvador Dali. Paul and Jane first met the Dalis at the New York home of Constance and Kirk Askew, a very wealthy couple who arranged literary and artistic dinner parties in the European style, a practice not at all common at the time. Paul remembers that when the butler approached Dali with the salad bowl, in the dimly lit dining-room, the young painter from Catalonia got very near the leaves of lettuce and, in an almost confidential tone, he said: 'They remind me of Swiss landscapes.' And he proceeded, in a serious and troubled voice, to tell the story of a poor Swiss girl, stranded in a snowstorm, whose face suddenly brightened when she saw a St Bernard approaching with a container of cognac at its neck. The thankful girl tried to embrace and kiss the huge dog, but the animal, totally rejecting her affection, devoured her.

The Bowleses' other encounters with Salvador Dali, who was always accompanied by Gala, took place with some frequency at the home of the Marquis of Cuevas who, at the time, dreamed of being the successor of Diaghilev. Even though he did not achieve this goal, one cannot deny his decisive contribution to contemporary ballet.

Oliver Smith, Paul's cousin and an excellent theatrical designer and promoter, was set on having the Marquis of Cuevas create a ballet with music by Paul and sets and costumes by Dali. And in fact he did. The original idea came from the Marquis himself and was based on a poem by Verlaine: 'Dans un vieux parc, solitaire et glacé. . . .' Paul was faithful to the poem's spirit and composed a score with light romantic touches. He did, however, make a fatal mistake: he attended only the orchestra rehearsals and did not go to the dance rehearsals with sets and costumes. When the curtain went up at the première in 1944 with all New York's *crème* in attendance, Paul was horrified at the spectacle. The dancers André Eglevsky and Marie-Jeanne appeared on-stage with hair extending from their armpits to the floor, and as if that weren't enough, several strange, tall, bearded men on bicycles circled the stage and occasionally collided with the dancers. In the midst of all this confusion there was a huge mechanical tortoise whose shell was composed of flashing coloured lights. The audience seemed to enjoy it, but Paul's music was barely audible. A colossal failure seemed likely, but that didn't happen, thanks to Salvador Dali's secret sway over a wealthy, 'snob' society that was really only partly 'cultured' and needed a shock now and again to reconfirm its cultural sophistication. At the end of the performance, Salvador and Gala, who were seated in front of Paul, turned round and said: 'It was just wonderful, don't you think?' The title of the ballet: 'Colloque Sentimental'.

Now I should like to recall two Spanish painters, exiles in New York, about whom Paul has surely forgotten yet both of whom have spoken to me (and very favourably) about Paul. The first,

Esteban (Esteve) Francés, was very grateful to Paul, for when Paul was on the editorial board of *View* he published a couple of cover designs and several illustrations in that journal, copies of which are today considered collectors' pieces. This surrealist painter of considerable merit forms part of the long list of forgotten figures who went into exile during the Franco dictatorship. Slowly some of these figures are being rediscovered.

The other painter who remembered Paul and his perfect Spanish was Luis Quintanilla, a good friend of Luis Buñuel and scion of an aristocratic family, who moved to Paris in 1912 to live a Bohemian life that turned out to be less than gilded. He achieved considerable fame as a muralist.

Julio (Juli) Ramis is an important Spanish painter whose role in the history of Spanish art has not been properly acknowledged. I myself took him to Paul's studio on Molière Street in Tangier. Despite his withdrawing, unsociable nature, Paul and he struck up an animated conversation about Joan Miró, whom he and Paul both admired. From then on Paul was interested in the development of his work.

In 1951 Tomás Seral y Casas invited Ramis to mount a show in Clan, that wonderful invention of his which, in addition to being a bookstore and art gallery, was a refuge for many young Spaniards who found Francoism simply repulsive. Among those young people were the most outstanding poets, novelists, painters and film directors of contemporary Spain. To the surprise of Seral and Ramis, Paul Bowles agreed to write a prologue for the book catalogue which was to be published in the series 'Colección de Artistas Nuevos', another invention/creation of Tomás y Seral and his wife, Gloria Aranda, both of whom are most unjustly forgotten by today's generation. This text was written in Spanish, in perfect Spanish, and Paul himself confessed to me that, except for a few pro-Trotsky pamphlets that he pasted like posters on Mexican walls in his youth, this was the first time that he dared to write a literary text in the language of Cervantes.

The following year, 1952, Paul returned to Madrid, for Ahmed Yacoubi was also going to have a show at Clan. Seral also published a book catalogue of Yacoubi's work in his 'Artistas Nuevos' collection, a series comprising thirteen volumes.

Finally, I must recall for Paul (and for myself) a painter whom both of us have known for more than fifty years. It may seem that I say this in jest, but, believe me, I am quite serious. I suspect that Paul will have guessed already to whom I am referring. Yes, it's Pablo Runyan, 'the most cosmopolitan of Panamanians', in the words of Margot Fonteyn. Through the years Pablo Runyan has told me innumerable anecdotes about his life and travels. He also likes other worlds, but not the solitude that Paul prizes. What Pablo likes is to plunge into the huge crowds in the great Eastern cities until he doesn't even remember where (or who) he is.

When Pablo Runyan arrived in New York after travelling the world as a sailor, he came under the always dangerous wing of Anaïs Nin. And one day, which he has never forgotten, he met Paul and Jane Bowles. He seems to remember (but is not entirely sure) that the events I am about to narrate took place in the 'Residencia de artistas' that George Davis, one of the editors of *Harper's Bazaar*, had founded in Brooklyn. He does remember clearly that Jerome Robbins was living there at the time. According to Pablo, Paul returned to the Residencia one afternoon with a bamboo cage, like the one Charlie Chan used in his films, with a fer de lance (that most poisonous of snakes) inside. Paul left the cage in the bathroom and immediately went to trap mice, since he had been told that they were the snake's favourite food.

When Paul returned, he discovered to his horror that the fer de lance had escaped from the bamboo cage. He spread the alarm through the building, and the residents began to search everywhere. While Paul was looking up and down, a scream was heard that left everyone paralysed with fear. It came from the lady who lived in the room beneath Paul's. Everyone ran downstairs, forced open the bathroom door, and discovered an elderly lady, nearly naked, seated on the toilet cover – nearer dead than alive! With great effort Paul moved her in her frozen state to the bed, and in the toilet-bowl he found the fer de lance, blissfully curled up in its humid refuge and totally oblivious of its mortal danger.

When I stop to think of the Hispanic writers I have heard Paul Bowles speak of, one name stands out above all the rest: Jorge Luis Borges. And it is only fair to point out that Paul's awareness of and admiration for Borges predated by many years his rise to fame thanks to Roger Caillois, who published the Argentinian's work in Gallimard's collection *La croix du sud*.

Paul has certainly read the most important Latin-American literary figures of his era. In Tangier he met Alejo Carpentier. Isabelle and Yvonne Gerofi gave a dinner for Alejo at Guitta's. There Paul met him and talked about the old days. Pilar Ibars and Eduardo Haro Tecglen were also with us.

Actually both Eduardito and Angel Vázquez were friends of Jane's. I can see them now emptying the water from the fishbowl, putting the fish in the sink and filling the fishbowl with the three bottles of champagne that Dr Roux had given Paul. Jane used to celebrate Sherifa's absences. She felt free and basked in that freedom, not matter how short-lived it was. I disagree with the biographies and literary portraits of Jane that are currently being written. They read like clinical charts: sickly, lesbian, embittered. . . . They did not know her. Even if one did know her, she defied classification. She never stopped surprising one. She could laugh at the world and at herself as only certain geniuses (most of them Jewish) have known how. And she was consumed by the flames of her own brilliance. Her work is a distant, pallid shadow of what she really was, perhaps because what she really was could not possibly be conveyed with words.

Angel Vázquez was born in Tangier in 1929 and died in Madrid in 1980. The first person to recognize his unique genius (and that's exactly what it was) was Jane Bowles who, long before his remarkable novel, *La vida perra de Juanita Narboni*, was published (he had previously published two other novels and a collection of stories), used to call him *mon petit génie rond*.

And to say farewell to my recollections, I cannot resist retelling for Paul one story that remains particularly in my memory.

One summer morning, opposite the Claridge café, I saw Jane go past looking distraught. I went up to her, and she almost began to cry as she told me that she had lost the key to her apartment, that Sherifa would not be able to get in and that she would create a big scene – and that it was all Paul's fault because he had gone away on a trip and left her by herself. I asked her if she had looked in her bag for the key, and she replied: 'I don't dare open it. . . .' On hearing this answer, I asked her to join me at a table at the rear of the Claridge. I spread the *Le Monde* I had just bought across the table, turned Jane's bag upside-down, and on to that improvised table-cloth fell the following items: a dead sparrow, a broken mirror, a comb, more than a few lentils – and key. Jane looked at me with excitement. Now we would have to resolve matters. The problem of the key was taken care of. We gathered the lentils in a handkerchief. In order to avoid bad luck, we decided to throw the broken mirror in the sea (which is what one should do in such cases), so we took a cab to the seafront. We buried the dead sparrow in a *terrain vague* near the Itesa building. Fortunately Sherifa was not seated on the stairs waiting for Jane when she returned. We went over to the Avenue España to have lunch on the terrace of the Bretagne. Jane was radiant and, much to my surprise, she began to sing 'Lazy Afternoon'. 'It's a song I'm very fond of. One of my best friends, John Latouche, wrote it. Isn't friendship wonderful?'

I shall always remember Jane like that: magical, brilliant, spurring our hopes and illusions, and laughing, forever laughing.

I shall always remember the day that Jane and I went down to the Main Zocco to confirm that the flower market had indeed disappeared. Jane burst into tears. Then she took my arm and when we saw that the old stone gate from the eleventh century had been covered with plaster and painted white, Jane shifted from tears to laughter. She said to me: 'Hollywood's Morocco is going to become the real Morocco', and then she added: 'Sherifa will no doubt be delighted by these changes.'

I must not end this piece without noting that Paul Bowles formed part of the first Committee in Defense of the Spanish Republic, which was organized in New York. More research needs to be done on the numerous committees formed in New York, Hollywood and other cities in the United States to defend the Republican cause. According to Luis Buñuel, the contributions of these committees – all of them private – were considerable. In 1937 the Federal Theater, following the lead of 'The Living Newspaper', produced a stage piece to publicize the reality of the conflict in Spain. The news arriving daily from Spain was announced and dramatized, and although it was a theatre of protest, it was based on very real events. The title of the work was: *Who Fights This Battle?* The text was by Kenneth White and the music by Paul Bowles.

Many years have gone by. Many years. Spain has regained its freedom, and in these new circumstances everything seems to have changed. When I see the works of Paul Bowles or posters with his photograph in the windows of bookshops, I say to myself: 'Paul, it's about time, don't you think?' And I know that he would answer me in Spanish, as he always has.

Stephen Spender

All I remember of Paul Bowles as a young man in Berlin is that he always seemed to be with Aaron Copland. I took it that he was studying composition with Copland. Christopher Isherwood and I thought of him as a potential composer and knew nothing of his writing. He had crinkly blond hair, and blue eyes, I seem to remember. He appears to have felt snubbed, or talked down to, by Christopher and me; and I am ashamed to say we may as English writers have treated this serious and quiet young American a bit *de haut en bas*.

Paul seems to have made friends with Christopher since then, but I don't think I have met him more than cursorily, subsequently.

Claude-Nathalie Thomas

A Translator's Experience

I first met Paul Bowles in 1973 at a dinner party in Tangier and immediately liked this soft-spoken, carefully dressed, courteous, blue-eyed American whose comments seemed to make sense. I had spent part of my childhood in the United States, but was living in Paris in strictly French surroundings and soon my main reason for coming to Morocco – I will now rather shamefacedly admit – was not to forge any particular link with the country, but to enjoy the privilege of brushing up on my English with educated expatriates or tourists, mostly writers and artists. They were an amusing lot, continually rushing to each other's houses to announce the birth of a new word such as 'quark' or 'quasar', which they had read in the *Herald Tribune* that morning. And the centre, the stable turning-point of their shifting universe seemed to be in Paul's obscure, plant-ridden apartment, where they claimed to find unexplained spiritual refreshment. After a while, some of them started pressing me to read Bowles's fiction.

By *The Delicate Prey*, I was swept into his enigmatic and ambiguous world – horrified, amused, overpowered by the clarity of vision, the truthfulness of detail. I suddenly found that my dreams were taking the form of short stories (or so it seemed for a brief instant on awakening), and since I had done some translations into French, I decided that Bowles's tales simply must find a French outlet. He and I made lists of likely stories, then I visited various publishers' offices and lent them that top-of-the-cream collection, *Pages from Cold Point*. But: 'No money to be made from short stories', came the boringly repetitious answer.

The time was not ripe. It would be another ten years or so before a journalist from the national daily *Libération*, looking for unusual material, came to me asking for Paul's address and for an introduction. He subsequently wrote a long article on Bowles which set the ball rolling in France. Now they scramble for the least drop of ink from the great man's pen.

Meanwhile, Paul – keen, I think, to be read by the French public – was patient with me. When a small young publisher decided to issue a collection of stories by Mohammed Mrabet, transcribed into English by Bowles from a tape in Moroccan Arabic, Paul suggested I do the French translation. Naïvely, I thought this would be good practice before working on Bowles's own style and after that I should find translating *Midnight Mass*, for instance, smooth sailing. How wrong I was! In opposition to Mrabet's characters, Bowles's don't simply do things, they think about them and react to them, sometimes through memories of what they formerly thought. And it becomes quite complicated when you want to choose the right terms to express all this in French.

Luckily, Paul is himself an expert translator and can usually help one out of a tough spot by suggesting – in English – an equivalent to what he wrote, if somewhat different in form. This generally sets me on the right track. Sometimes, though, his explanations can be puzzling. Once, I asked him what a certain character meant by a statement he had made, and the startling answer came: 'Why, nothing. Nothing at all. He's just trying to hide what he's really thinking. . . .'

Paul is extraordinarily precise and he won't let mistakes in a character's point of view slip into a translation if he gets a chance to read it. At times, he will spend hours correcting others' errors in punctuation and typing. By his generosity in criticism, I believe he has helped many people. I feel fortunate to have been one of them.

Gore Vidal

Paul Bowles's Stories

'Carson McCullers, Paul Bowles, Tennessee Williams are, at this
moment at least, the three most interesting writers in the United
States.' A third of a century has passed since I wrote that sentence
in a piece on contemporary American writing.

Later, when I reprinted those words, I felt obliged to add: 'This
was written in 1952. McCullers was a good and fashionable novelist
of the day (I cannot say that I have any great desire to read her
again). Paul Bowles was as little known then as he is now. His short
stories are among the best ever written by an American. Tennessee
Williams, etc. . . .' All in all, I still see no reason not to support my
youthful judgement of Paul Bowles. As a short-story writer, he has
had few equals in the second half of the twentieth century. Obvious
question: If he is so good, why is he so little known?

Great American writers are supposed not only to live in the
greatest country in the world (the United States, for those who
came in late), but to write about that greatest of all human themes:
the American experience. From the beginning of the Republic, this
crude America First-ism has flourished. As a result, there is a
strong tendency to misrepresent or undervalue our three finest
novelists: Henry James (who lived in England), Edith Wharton
(who lived in France), Vladimir Nabokov (who lived in Switzerland, and who wasn't much of an American anyway despite an
unnatural passion for our motels, so lyrically rendered in *Lolita*).

Paul Bowles has lived most of his life in Morocco. He seldom
writes about the United States. On the other hand, he has shrewd
things to say about Americans confronted with strange cultures
and . . . strange selves.

Born in 1910, Bowles was brought up in New York City and
New England. He attended the University of Virginia. When he
was seventeen, the Paris-based avant-garde magazine *transition*

published some of his poems. Bowles went to Paris, met Gertrude Stein, was influenced by the Surrealists. He quit school to become a writer. Except for Poe, his writing derives not from the usual Anglo-American tradition but from such 'exotics' as Valéry, Roussel, Gide and, of course, the expatriate Miss Stein. Later, he was to put to his own uses oral Mexican and Moroccan folklore; he listened as much as he read.

I suspect that Bowles's apparent foreignness has limited the number of doctoral theses that ought by now to have been devoted to one whose art far exceeds that of . . . well, name the great American writers of our day (a list that was as different yesterday as it will be tomorrow). For the American academic, Bowles is still odd man out; he writes as if *Moby Dick* had never been written. Odder still, he is also a distinguished composer of music. In fact, he supported himself for many years by writing incidental music for such Broadway plays as *The Glass Menagerie*. It is curious that at a time when a number of serious critics have expressed the hope that literature might one day take on the attributes of the 'highest' of all the arts, music, Bowles has been composing music as well as writing prose. I am certain that the first critic able to deal both with his music and his writing will find that Bowles's life work has been marvellous in a way not accessible to those of us who know only one or the other of the two art forms. Only Anthony Burgess knows enough to do him justice.

In 1972 Paul Bowles wrote a memoir called *Without Stopping*. For those able to read between the lines, the book was pleasurable. For anyone else, it must have sounded a bit like Julius Caesar's account of the wars in Gaul. Although there is a good deal of information about various commanders and troop movements, we don't learn much about what the subject had in mind. But there are interesting asides, and the best sort of memoir is entirely to one side of the mere facts of a life.

We learn that Bowles originally wanted to be a writer, not a composer. But at a progressive school he had shown an aptitude for mathematics, cousin germane to music. Nevertheless, he preferred to arrange words rather than notes upon a page until Gertrude Stein read his poems. 'She sat back and thought a moment. Then she said: "Well, the only trouble with all this is that it isn't poetry."' She found his images false; did not think much of his attempt to write in the surreal manner, 'without conscious intervention'. Later, she asked him if he had rewritten the poems. When he said no, 'She was triumphant. "You see," she cried. "I told you you were no poet. A real poet, after one conversation, would have gone upstairs and at least tried to recast them, but you haven't even looked at them."' Bowles stopped writing. He turned to music.

Between 1929 and 1945 he made a name as a composer. He married the odd, brilliant Jane Bowles. She was a writer. He was a composer. Together and separately, they were much admired. During the late thirties and forties they became central figures in the transatlantic (and pan-American) world of the arts. Although unknown to the general public, the Bowleses were famous among those who were famous; and in some mysterious way the art grandees wanted, if not the admiration of the Bowleses (seldom bestowed), their tolerance.

They lived in Mexico (the unknown Tennessee Williams made a pilgrimage to their house in Acapulco); they lived in New York, sharing a house with W.H. Auden and Benjamin Britten. After the Second World War they moved for good to Tangier, where Paul Bowles still lives. Jane Bowles died in Spain in 1973.

In the spring of 1945 Charles Henri Ford asked Bowles to edit an issue of the magazine *View*. The subject was Central and South American culture. Bowles translated a number of Spanish writers, and wrote some texts of his own. In the course of 'reading some ethnographic books with texts from the Arapesh or from the Tarahumara given in word-for-word translation . . . the desire came to me to invent my own myths, adopting the point of view of the primitive mind'. He resorted to 'the old Surrealist method of abandoning conscious control and writing whatever words came from the pen'. The first of these stories was written 'one rainy Sunday'; it is called 'The Scorpion'.

The story was well received, and Bowles went on writing. 'The subject-matter of the myths soon turned from "primitive" to contemporary. . . . It was through this unexpected little gate that I crept back into the land of fiction writing. Long ago I had decided that the world was too complex for me ever to be able to write fiction; since I failed to understand life, I would not be able to find points of reference which the hypothetical reader might have in common with me.' He did not entirely proceed through that small gate until he wrote 'A Distant Episode' and found that if life was no more understandable to him than before, prose was. He now possessed the art to depict his dreams.

During the next thirty years Paul Bowles wrote thirty-nine short stories. They were published originally in three volumes: *The Delicate Prey* (1950); *The Time of Friendship* (1967); *Things Gone and Thing Still Here* (1977). Even before the first collection was published, three of the stories caused a great stir in the literary world. 'Pages from Cold Point', 'The Delicate Prey' and 'A Distant Episode' were immediately recognized as being unlike anything else in our literature. I have just reread the three stories, with some nervousness. After all these years, I wondered if they would still 'work'. In my youth I had admired D.H. Lawrence's novels. Now, I deeply dislike them. I was relieved to find that Bowles's art is still as disturbing as ever. I was surprised to note how the actual stories differ from my memory of them. I recalled a graphic description of a sixteen-year-old boy's seduction of his father on a hot summer night in Jamaica. Over the years, carnal details had built up in my memory like a coral reef. Yet on rereading 'Pages from Cold Point', nothing (and everything) happens. In his memoirs Bowles refers, rather casually, to this story as something he wrote aboard ship from New York to Casablanca: 'a long story about a hedonist . . .' It is a good deal more than that. Both 'The Delicate Prey' and 'A Distant Episode' create the same sense of strangeness and terror that they did the first time I read them. 'The Delicate Prey' turns on a Gidean *acte gratuit*: the slicing off of the boy's penis is not only like the incident on the train in *Les caves du Vatican* but also presages the driving of a nail through a skull in Bowles's novel *Let It Come Down*. 'A Distant Episode' seems to me to be more than ever emblematic of the helplessness of an overcivilized sensibility (the professor's) when confronted with an alien culture. Captured by North African nomads, his tongue cut out, he is made into a clown, a toy. He is used to make his captors laugh. He *appears* to accept his fate. Something harsh is glimpsed in the lines of a story that is now plainer in its reverberations than it was when written. But then it is no longer news to anyone that the floor to this ramshackle civilization that we have built cannot bear our weight much longer. It was Bowles's genius to suggest the horrors which lie beneath that floor, as fragile, in its way, as the sky that shelters us from a devouring vastness.

The stories fall into rough categories. First: locale. Mexico and North Africa are the principal settings. Landscape is all-important in a Bowles story. Second: how the inhabitants of alien cultures regard the creatures of our civilized world, as in 'Under the Sky'. Bowles goes even further in a beautiful story called 'The Circular Valley' where human life is depicted as it must appear to the anima of a place. This spirit inhabits at will those human beings who visit its valley; feeds on their emotions; alters them during its occupancy. Third: the stories of transference. In 'You Are Not I' a madwoman becomes her sane sister. In 'Allal' a boy exchanges personality with a snake. The intensity of these stories makes them more like waking dreams than so many words on a page. Identity is transferred in such a way that one wonders which, finally, is which? And what is what? The effect is rather like the Taoist story of the man who dreamed that he was a butterfly. When 'he woke up with a start, he did not know whether he was Chuang Chou who had dreamed that he was a butterfly, or whether he was a butterfly dreaming that he was Chuang Chou. Between Chuang Chou and the butterfly there must be some distinction. This is what is called the transformation of things'.

There are a number of more or less realistic stories that deal with the plain incomprehension of Americans in contact with the natives of Mexico, North Africa, Thailand. One of the most amusing is 'You Have Left Your Lotus Pods on the Bus'. An American goes on an excursion with some Buddhist priests. The day is filled with splendid misunderstandings. There is the man at the back of a crowded bus who never stops screaming. He is ignored by everyone except the American who wonders why no one shuts him up. At the end, the priests tell him that the 'madman' is an employee of the bus company giving necessary warnings and advice to the driver.

In several stories white ladies respond not-so-ambiguously to dark-skinned youths. Bowles notes the sadism that sexual frustration can cause ('At Paso Rojo'). But where the ordinary writer would leave it at that, Bowles goes deeper into the human case and, paradoxically, he achieves his greatest effects when he concentrates entirely on surfaces. Although he seldom describes a human face, he examines landscape with the precision of a geologist. Bowles himself seems like one of those bright, sharp-eyed birds that flit from story to story, staring with eyes that do not blink at desert, hills, sky. He records weather with all the solemnity of a meteorologist. He looks closely at food. As for his human characters, he simply lets them reveal themselves through what they say or do not say. Finally, he is a master of suggesting anxiety (Are all the traveller's cheques lost or just mislaid?) and dread (Will this desert prove to be the setting for a very special death?). Story after story turns on flight. It is no accident that Bowles called his memoir (with pride?) *Without Stopping*.

Four stories were written to demonstrate that by using 'kif-inspired motivations, the arbitrary would be made to seem natural, the diverse elements could be fused, and several people would automatically become one'. These pieces strike me as entirely uninhabited, and of no interest. Yet in other stories (inspired perhaps by smaller doses of kif) he does demonstrate the essential oneness of the many as well as the interchangeability not only of personality but of all things. As Webster saw the skull beneath the skin, so Bowles has glimpsed what lies back of our sheltering sky . . . an endless flux of stars so like those atoms which make us up that in our apprehension of this terrible infinity, we experience not only horror but likeness.

Terry Wilson

Tangier 90

It took awhile for us to find the Immeuble Itesa. We, Philippe Baumont and I, were in Tangier as representatives of a fabled European arts foundation. As far as we were concerned, we were there to arrange a showing of Brion Gysin's last Big Picture, the *Makemono*, but naturally, in the circumstances, we found ourselves subjected to opposition and support from all manner of interested parties. . . . The Moroccan undercover cop out of a Marx Brothers movie – sometimes a moustache, sometimes not – got right on to the job and resorted to poison without further ado. After that, having laid us both out for about twenty-four hours of continual vomiting, he seemed content to observe comings and goings from the hotel lounge, with or without his moustache. The French and Americans opened their doors and their ears. Gavin Young was in town.

Also on hand were the incomparable Hamri and, of course, the practically immortal David Herbert. Expected imminently were Ira Cohen, long-time Bowles *amigo*, and his son Raphael, who were to complete our somewhat motley crew.

Anyway, after we managed to get up off the floor we tottered down the stairs past the cop and out, heading for the Itesa, Calle Campoamor, on the western outskirts – totally nondescript, totally anonymous, this is the way, all the way up to the top floor. There is no phone. You just drop round. I give the door a tap and a couple of raps. Eventually it opens and Mrabet, small, poker-faced, wiry, somnolent, lets us in. Through the foyer stacked high with worn leather suitcases and trunks and into the salon. I have with me a Swedish magazine with a Bowles interview I imagine Paul may not have seen, but he has and immediately launches into a complaint about the interviewer who has apparently also broken into print expressing dismay at the austerity of his living conditions. Paul is not amused, as if somehow I am responsible. This is amusing, since the same writer had previously given my place the once-over – 'the mysteriously bulging walls, the permanent deep chill no heater can quite dispel', etc. Paul has about three and a half rooms up there. No doubt Howard Hughes would have found it a bit hairy, but Paul is quite comfortable. He has lived in this apartment since the late fifties and in Tangier of course longer than practically anyone – with the exception of David Herbert, I suppose.

Paul was generally confined to bed during the period of our visit and was more or less content, especially after Ira arrived, to sit back and listen, frail, white-haired, bright-eyed, benignly bemused. We talk about Brion – '*Cut-ups!*' I said: 'You're *crazy!*' Paul is exclaiming – as the apartment slowly fills up, as it does every day, these days, with a succession of camera crews, journalists, old friends, new friends. When someone remarks on Paul's apparent light-heartedness, he smiles back. 'That's because I'm in pain.' A typical Bowles response. Ira says that when he asked Paul why he wrote his poignant and obviously deeply felt poem 'Next to Nothing' (originally published by Ira in Nepal), he replied: 'Because you asked me.' The old names hover in the air . . . Brion . . . Alfred . . . Yacoubi . . . Sherifa, Jane, 'existing only in the minds of us who remember'. The lights flicker. I amble back through the smoky salon, to find Mrabet locked eyeball to dilated eyeball with a fat young American film-maker, a confrontation between Fu Manchu and Humpty Dumpty. 'At least his first few little cheques were good,' Mrabet seems to be rasping. Back into the bedroom, Phillip Ramey is there, Abdelouahaid, Paul's driver, Raphael, Ira . . . 'Truman' . . . 'Alfred' . . . 'Yacoubi' . . . 'Jane' . . . 'Sherifa' . . 'Brion'. . . .

'And when our lines have been cut as well, we shall all be a part of the same *grand néant*. Even that consoling thought isn't of much help. . . .'

The lights have blown but the names still hover.

Gavin Young

Strange to think that I once thought the delightful, though determinedly pessimistic author of *The Sheltering Sky* frightening enough for me to want to avoid meeting him at all costs. Now, from one week to another, I look forward eagerly to his appearances at luncheon at my rented house – usually Abdul Latif's couscous at Paul's own request.

The first year I spent any time in Tangier I never met Paul Bowles. He had been living there a few years by then, in 1957, and from somewhere I had acquired a neurotic suspicion he would scare the pants off me. I imagined, I think, a terrifyingly intellectual hippie; long-haired, bearded, impatient of my English accent; habitually spaced out by the local drug, kif, in contemptuous rage at anyone who could not have written *The Naked Lunch*, or something mighty like it. It was, after all, the pre-Orton period in Tangier, of Burroughs, Capote and Tennessee Williams.

My literary 'coterie', if I can presume to call him that, consisted merely of one person I hoped would advise me on a paying profession; on a life that would not take me back to London and confine me behind an office desk for the rest of time. Ian Fleming, then struggling in Tangier's El Minzah Hotel to turn James Bond into a money-spinner, was a more down-to-earth companion. Apart from his life with Bond, Ian was Foreign Editor of the London *Sunday Times* and I took his advice and became a foreign correspondent. It was nearly thirty years before I visited Tangier again.

Paul had changed his residence by 1985; he had lived alone since his wife, Jane, died some time before. I had imagined on that first visit that they lived in a certain grand Bohemian way somewhere in the bazaar – and maybe they had done. This time I was brave enough to call.

Nothing was as I had imagined. Paul inhabited – and inhabits –

the fourth floor of a block of flats which, if not exactly seedy, was certainly nothing to write home about. A ring at the bell brought such a prolonged silence that I imagined the thing was out of order. When at last the door slowly opened, there was Mr Bowles himself, peeking through the crack. Nervously I introduced myself – I had not been able to telephone in advance of my arrival, since Paul (typically) does not run to a telephone – and at once he stepped graciously aside, saying 'Come in, come in' in tones that were unmistakably genial.

That was the first pleasant surprise. The second was to see, in place of the pugnacious, long-haired Bohemian with dilated pupils I had imagined – a sort of knock-'em-down Ezra Pound – someone of a quite different kind. I should have known. I had seen photographs of Paul's friend, the author of *The Naked Lunch*, William Burroughs, and been surprised at his suit and tie and the waistcoat he habitually wore. It was not the sort of outfit I expected 'decadent' writers to wear. Though in no way decadent, Virgil Thomson, the American composer and critic, who I knew was a friend of Paul's in their Gertrude Stein-Paris days (when Paul was composing, too) and whom I saw regularly in New York, was never to be seen without a three-piece suit, a watch-chain, and a correct third of an inch of cuff at the wrist. I should have guessed that Paul might be of the same fastidiously dressed American mould. His clothes, I could see immediately, were all of the best material (overcoat by Dunhill, I noticed), and he wore plenty of them. In fact, on this particularly warm Moroccan day, he was wearing not only the overcoat but a sweater and I suspected long johns as well. 'Cold day, isn't it?' he said mildly. I agreed, surreptitiously wiping sweat from my brow, and he offered me tea.

Paul dresses as though he lives in a permanent snowstorm. His flat is made unusually chilly and dark by dusty clusters of vegetation in the window that prevent the least sunlight from penetrating. There is no view to speak of anyway. The walls are lined with books, and in winter – Morocco has a bitter winter – Paul takes refuge in the bed, not a very big one, which fills most of a second room. Sometimes he takes his meals to bed with him and eats huddled in shawls. In the street on chilly days, similarly huddled, he reminds me of some small mammal anxiously hibernating. How he survives the winters, if he finds the summers so cold, I shall never know.

Since that day, I have seen a lot of Paul – although not nearly enough. Occasionally I rent a house on a mountain. It has a garden and when the summer sun is out Paul comes to lunch. There is a swing in the garden – not so much of a real 'swing', actually, as a rubber car type hanging on a rope from the branch of a weeping willow – and Paul likes to be pushed back and forth in it by my Moroccan servant.

Watching this, I ask myself if this is the Paul Bowles I had fearfully avoided all those years ago, a merrily giggling Paul whose only fear seems to be that, if things are going well and the sun is out, some disaster, by that very fact, must be imminent. I have never known a human being who so mistrusts happiness. The wonder is that mistrust doesn't put the kibosh on his delightful sense of humour. He is a quietly wonderful talker when he gets going, and a very precise one who takes time to select the exact word in the context. This may sound pedantic, but the effect is to make everything he says sound unusually . . . reliable.

Paul must be abnormally patient with – or, perhaps more realistically, abnormally tolerant of – bores. Since he has no telephone, the unending stream of pilgrims to his flat – they come unbidden from America, France, from everywhere – are unable to give warning of their arrival. Not that many of these importunates would think of affording their guru such a courtesy. These total strangers batter at his door at all hours. I often wonder if, as I was, they are astonished by what they find: a small, neat, well-dressed, perfectly mannered, rather conservative man with a soft voice and short, well-tended white hair, in place of what I suppose they expected – a loud and rather crude old geezer, hippie high priest, fragrant with kif, who, once their recording machines are in motion (most of them carry the damned things), will turn on a well-rehearsed stream of outrageous Joycean instructions for 'dropping out'.

Whatever they expect, I am quite sure they do not anticipate the gentle, rather puzzled-looking man I am delighted to see every week for lunch at my rented house on the hill, eyeing through the window with a certain wistful longing the rubber tyre under the weeping willow, as though fearful it will vanish, as for him all good things continually threaten to, before he can get to it.

He needn't worry. In a moment Abdul Latif and I will give the author of *Let It Come Down*, one of the least alarming writers I have ever met, the swing he enjoys so much. Then – laughing merrily, and muffled and scarfed as if for a snap midsummer blizzard, not all that far from the red-hot sandy steppers of the Algerian Sahara of *The Sheltering Sky*, the Atlas Mountains and airless mysterious Fez of *The Spider's Web*, and within plain sight of the warm Mediterranean blue of the Strait of Gibraltar – Paul Bowles will fly gaily through the air, while Abdul Latif's three-year-old son, and Sam, the household mongrel, look on with a wild surmise.

About the Contributors

Francis Bacon, arguably the greatest painter of his generation, died in 1992.

Melvyn Bragg, novelist and broadcaster, is executive producer of London Weekend Television's *The South Bank Show* and presenter of BBC's *Start the Week* on Radio 4. Mr Bragg has interviewed Paul Bowles for his television programme.

William S. Burroughs' novel *The Naked Lunch*, first published in Britain by John Calder, was recently filmed by David Cronenberg. Mr Burroughs now lives in Lawrence, Kansas.

John Cage was one of the twentieth century's leading composers. He is also the author of *Empty Words, For the Birds, Silence, A Year From Monday, M: Writings 1962–72* and *X: Writings 1979–1982* (all published by Marion Boyars).

Ira Cohen travelled to Tangier in 1965, when he published *Gnaoua*. In 1970 he moved to the Himalayas, where he published the work of Paul Bowles, Gregory Corso and Charles Henri Ford. An exhibition of his photography and other works has held recently at the October Gallery, London. Ira Cohen lives now in New York City.

Gregory Corso divides his time between New York and Rome. His Beat poetry includes *Gasoline* and *Bomb*.

Anne Cumming has been dubbed 'the randy granny' by the *News of the World* and, at the age of 74, has posed topless for the *Sunday Sport*. She lived for many years in Rome, working in the Italian film industry. She is the author of *The Love Habit* and *The Love Quest* (published by Peter Owen) and is currently writing a travel book, *Destination Romance: Men on Five Dollars a Day*.

Millicent Dillon's biography of Jane Bowles, *A Little Original Sin*, appeared in 1991 (Virago Press). She is at work on a book about Paul Bowles.

Ruth Fainlight's books include *Sibylle and Others, Fifteen to Infinity, Selected Poems* and *The Knot* (all published by Hutchinson). Her libretto

The Dancer Hotoke, performed at Covent Garden, was short-listed for a Laurence Olivier Award. Ms Fainlight is married to the novelist Alan Sillitoe.

Lawrence Ferlinghetti, Beat poet, is the author of many books, including *Pictures of the Gone World*, *A Coney Island of the Mind* and *Love in the Days of Rage*. For many years he has been the motivating force behind City Lights, booksellers, publishers and a cultural beacon in San Francisco.

Charles Henri Ford lives in Crete, Paris, New York and Kathmandu. When his book *The Young and Evil* (co-authored with Parker Tyler) was published by Obelisk Press in 1933, the British Customs and Excise, in their wisdom, seized and burnt all 500 copies. The book has recently been reissued by Gay Men's Press.

Allen Ginsberg is perhaps the most famous of the Beat poets. His poetry includes *Howl* and *Kaddish*.

The Hon. David Herbert grew up at Wilton House as the second son of the Earl of Pembroke. He has lived in Tangier for over forty years and has written three volumes of reminiscences: *Second Son*, *Engaging Eccentrics* and *Relations and Revelations: Advice to Jemima* (all published by Peter Owen). The last book includes a Foreword by Paul Bowles, who says of him: 'He wants to know every kind of person there is, and in his house one is likely to meet just about that'.

Patricia Highsmith has said of Paul Bowles that 'he engages a reader with prose of flat honesty, while leading him into dark alleys where he may not want to go'. Hitchcock filmed her *Strangers on a Train*. Her most recent books are the re-issued *Carol* and *Ripley Under Water*, set partly in Morocco. Patricia Highsmith lives now in Switzerland.

John Hopkins, author of *Tangier Buzzless Flies*, made Morocco his home for seventeen years; he now lives in some style in a restored vicarage in Oxfordshire. His most recent novel is *In the Chinese Mountains* (Peter Owen), and is set in the mountains of Peru.

Buffie Johnson has been a member of the avant-garde for as long as anyone can remember. She is an internationally known abstract-expressionist painter and her recently published book, *Lady of the Beasts*, has become a classic of its genre. Over the last ten years she has spent her summers in Tangier, staying in Jane Bowles's old apartment below Paul's. She has known Paul Bowles for fifty years.

Gavin Lambert's novel *Inside Daisy Clover* was filmed in 1965, with a cast that included Natalie Wood, Robert Redford, Ruth Gordon and Christopher Plummer. His screenplays include *Sons and Lovers* and *The Roman Spring of Mrs Stone*.

Nicholas Lezard is a young journalist based in London.

Marguerite McBey, widow of the Scottish painter James McBey, spends a good part of every year in Tangier, where she lived for many years. She has painted both Paul and Jane Bowles. Her most recent exhibition was held at the Fine Arts Society, London, in 1992.

Peter Owen's eponymous independent publishing house celebrated its fortieth anniversary in 1991, when Francis Bacon hailed its founder as 'the only publisher in England who produces anything interesting'. Peter Owen is the author of *Publishing: The Future* (1988) and *The Peter Owen Anthology* (1991).

Gary Pulsifer has worked in publishing on both sides of the Atlantic and as Literature Officer at the Riverside Studios in West London. He published Desmond Hogan's novel *The Ikon Maker* under the imprint of Pulsifer Press. He is now in the employ of the above-named Mr Owen.

James Purdy is considered as 'an authentic American genius' by Gore Vidal. His latest novel, *Out with the Stars*, is published by Peter Owen, as are his other works of fiction; he is also the author of plays and poetry, which appear under the imprint of Athenaeum, Amsterdam. James Purdy lives in Brooklyn, New York.

Phillip Ramey is an American composer, pianist and writer. His output encompasses orchestral and chamber pieces, including a large body of piano music. His most recent works are *Concerto No. 3 for Piano and Orchestra* and *Tangier Portraits for Piano*. Since 1977 he has been the annotator and programme editor of the New York Philharmonic Orchestra.

Richard Rayner, former Books Editor of *Time Out*, is the author of *Los Angeles Without a Map* and a novel, *The Elephant* (Picador). He has been described as 'the freshest and most startling new voice in years' (US *Vogue*) and 'an exuberant storyteller' (*Daily Telegraph*).

Edouard Roditi, who died in May 1992, was a celebrated poet, translator, biographer and author of short stories.

Ned Rorem, composer and writer, numbers among his publications *The Paris and New York Diaries*, *The Later Diaries*, and *The Nantucket Diary 1973–1985*.

John Ryle has worked as an anthropologist in southern Sudan. He is an Area Consultant to the Save the Children Fund for north-east Africa. Formerly Foreign Editor of the *Times Literary Supplement*, he is currently writing a book about Brazil.

Lady St Just is literary executor of the Tennessee Williams Estate. Her edition of *Five o'Clock Angel: The Letters of Tennessee Williams to Maria St Just* has been published to wide acclaim in Britain, the United States and France; it will shortly appear in a Korean edition.

Emilio Sanz de Soto is a noted Spanish writer.

Sir Stephen Spender's novel *The Temple* appeared in 1988; a paperback edition of his *Journals* has appeared recently, as well as *Hockney's Alphabet*, which he edited (all Faber & Faber).

Claude-Nathalie Thomas has translated into French Paul Bowles's books *Midnight Mass*, *Up Above the World* and *The Spider's House*. She has also translated *Plain Pleasures* by Jane Bowles and Mohammed Mrabet's *M'Hashish*.

Gore Vidal is one of America's most celebrated writers. His many books include *The City and the Pillar*, *Myra Breckinbridge*, *Washington D.C.*, *Lincoln*, *Duluth* and, most recently, *Live from Golgotha*.

Terry Wilson is the co-author with Brion Gysin of *Here to Go* (Quartet Books, UK and Re/Search, US). His other books are *D-Train* (Grapheme), *Dreams of Green Base* (Inkblot), and two recently completed titles, *The Nervous System* and *The Perilous Passage*.

Gavin Young wrote for *The Observer* for many years and is still associated with that newspaper. His highly praised travel books include *Slow Boat to China*; his biography *In Search of Conrad* was published in 1992.